Moving From Within

Moving from Within

A New Method for Dance Making

Alma M. Hawkins

a cappella books

Library of Congress Cataloging-in-Publication Data

Hawkins, Alma M.
   Moving from within: a new method for dance making/ by Alma
M. Hawkins. — 1st ed.
      p.   cm.
   Includes bibliographical references.
   ISBN 1-55652-139-1 : $12.95
   1. Choreography. 2. Modern dance—Study and teaching.
3. Creative ability. I. Title.
GV1782.5.H4 1991   91-29851
792.8'2—dc20   CIP

Printed in the United States of America
   5 4 3 2 1

Published 1991 by a cappella books, incorporated

Editorial offices:
PO Box 380
Pennington, NJ 08535

Business/sales offices:
814 N. Franklin St.
Chicago, IL 60610

Photographs of students at the UCLA and Santa Monica
College Departments of Dance by William Ericson and
Anthony Hall.

Contents

Acknowledgments

I wish to express my appreciation to the students who participated in the choreography project and provided a constant source of inspiration; to Linda Gold who made the experimental project possible in the dance program at Santa Monica College; to Marian Scott who read an early draft of the manuscript and made valuable suggestions; and to Alice, my sister, who listened and shared ideas throughout this writing project.

Foreword

Creativity is a private affair. It is the process of rummaging through and penetrating the intimate world of accumulated memories, thoughts, and sensations down to the very nature of being. If the process of creating does not begin at the source, it stands the danger of becoming a surface experience resulting in a superficial display.

To reach into this illusive world and draw forth a created entity seems an almost impossible task to be undertaken from the outside. After all, who knows yourself better than you? Who best knows how to reach your richest center, best knows how to interpret the intricate morass that constitutes you?

There is a specific creativity and general creativity. The first is an act of you and the God in you. The latter is a process that leads you into the formidable presence of that deity within yourself.

The language of internal sensory communication is only in part a verbal language. Images, sensations, obscurities, emotions, intuitions, and biological factors are all involved in the internal communication system, so that words alone, both written and spoken, are inadequate and present limitations. Words and their definitions are the greatest obstacles to comprehension. The most literally specific definition can be misconstrued as it passes through the filter of your personality.

Anthropologists speculate that at an early stage of human

development, the gift of speech did not exist and that tribes communicated intuitively through a central bank of experiences that were common to all. Though descriptive imagery was limited, the participation with that experience was deeper. Perhaps it is this inner language that artists have inherited and maintained over time that gives them the distinction of aesthetic depth.

Words can shift swiftly from ally to adversary. An inflection can easily alter an intention, and yet words are our common means of teaching and communicating.

In addition to what is being said is the equally important manifestation of how it is written. The written word reveals only a partial meaning of itself. Its meaning becomes fuller when it is spoken and heard and completed with experience. Therefore a book such as this, which ranges so freely through narrative, lesson plan, philosophy, and influence, must be met halfway by the reader. If read merely as words, it will miss its mark. It must talk to you with all the persuasion of a good teacher making a point or creating an environment in which to operate. The words must assume a depth of meaning as well as their two-dimensional presence on the page.

Many books have been written about the process of creativity. However, what distinguishes one from the other is its author. It is important to know something about Alma Hawkins because the validity of this book rests upon her reputation and experience, and how her many years of specialization and work in the field of dance education endows her with a distinctive authority.

Alma aptly demonstrated her knowledge and participation in the many facets of the art during her long tenure as administrator of dance at UCLA. The biological and psychological factors of the body, the theatrical aspects of production and music, teaching and mentoring students and colleagues, all became a matter of daily activity to her. She is enormously respected for her wholehearted dedication to the field of dance. She has addressed every level of dance from a book on composition for high-school age students, to consultations and pertinent private meetings with the great artists in the field. All in all, dance is her life, and, after her retirement from UCLA, it was her commitment to dance that brought her to the question of creativity as a specific personal process.

At Santa Monica College, she had the opportunity to work with more experienced dance students. For five years she tried and developed methods to reach and unlock the door behind which there rested and lurked the beast guarding the identity of self. Her students were not bound by the precocious drive of professional dance performance, but were concerned instead with creativity and dance on their own level.

One must imagine as one reads this book the steady, comforting, and guiding voice that spoke the lines, directed the actions, and urged her students to probe and reveal.

This book is about a process. A process to encourage experience. That is why I say it must be met halfway. It must be brought to life and not just read as words and ideas.

Many people, particularly during this last century, have written about creativity. This book bares Alma Hawkins' unique wisdom and conclusions. It is written as part philosophy, part psychology, and part lesson plan, all of which must be considered when reading and presenting this material.

Creativity will long remain a mystery. We can only hope that the mystery will be challenged. However, creativity is not something to be answered or solved. It is the continual process of discovery. Creativity and mystery are essential to life. Studying creativity and its mysterious origins is a process that will bring us closer to them both: a process pertinent to who we are and what we know about ourselves.

Murray Louis

Introduction

Throughout my many years of teaching, I have always been interested in creativity and movement as a means of experiencing and expressing. During my years at UCLA, when I had the opportunity to work with undergraduate and graduate dance majors, my goal was to assist individuals in developing their creative potential and understanding of dance as an art form. During that time, I was searching constantly for new ways to facilitate creative growth.

Intertwined with my teaching in the dance department was ten years of experience working with emotionally disturbed adults and children in a psychiatric institution. My focus in that situation was on the creative use of movement as a means of facilitating individual change and growth. In other words, movement was used as a means of therapeutic intervention. It was through this work with patients that I discovered the true meaning of basic or organic movement as a vital force in the living process. Though I had long been interested in creativity, it was at this time that I started searching for a deeper understanding of the creative process. I wanted to know more about the nature of the process and the metaphoric use of movement to create dance forms.

In recent years, I have had the opportunity to concentrate on an experimental approach to the teaching of choreography. I undertook this new teaching venture with college dance students because

I wanted to explore my ideas about a basic human process that I believe supports the creative life of the individual. Also, I wanted to test the validity of a new approach to choreography in an ongoing teaching-learning environment.

My motivation for undertaking this project was reinforced by my concern about what is happening in much of our contemporary dance. Certainly some of the choreography seen today is brilliant and aesthetically satisfying, but all too frequently this is not the case. Often we leave the theater with a feeling of wanting more. The dances may be well crafted and skillfully performed, but one is not moved by the experience. We find ourselves becoming viewers of technical feats, costumes, lighting design, and patterns of movement unrelated to any inner substance; art is more than that. The movement event should have the power to evoke an aesthetic response. What is it about a piece of choreography that causes the audience to be drawn into the experience, to respond imaginatively, and to feel aesthetic satisfaction?

This book grows out of my search for an answer to that question. The focus in the following chapters is on a way of working, a way of facilitating a learning environment that encourages individuals to develop their creative potential and frees them to experience, to discover, and to give external form to their inner vision. The emphasis is on process rather than product. My belief is that when the young artist has a clear motivation and is deeply involved in the process, the externalized dance event will take shape and have its own form.

The question confronting the teacher is: How do we create experiences that help the young choreographer create works that are substantive and aesthetically satisfying? Do we try to pass on knowledge and experience that has been codified, or do we provide an enriched environment that motivates individuals to be self-directed and to make their own discoveries? It seems to me that we must take the latter approach, if we are interested in helping individuals develop their ability to use movement as a means of making dance forms that reflect their own unique experience.

Though we usually think of a choreography class as a place of doing and making, I believe that there is a real need to find a more holistic approach to learning. Along with the doing and making, the student needs enriching experiences that contribute to an increased understanding of creativity, of art forms, and of the experience of artists in various media.

Nurturing the creative potential of the young choreographer requires both structure and freedom: *structure* in the sense of a framework that encourages the discovery of concepts and truths related to the artistic process; *freedom* in the sense of the opportunity to explore movement ideas and allow the imaginative transformation of experiences (inner vision) to take shape in an externalized form. The challenge is to provide a structure and learning environment that facilitates growth and at the same time protects the individual's freedom to take a hand in his or her own creative development and pursue personal goals with self-confidence.

The purpose of this book is to present a way of working that is based on concepts of creativity and the use of imagery in an integrated approach to learning. My hope is that the findings of my seven years of experimental teaching (five years in a fundamentals of choreography course and two years with a mentor group) will be useful to others who are seeking new approaches to artistic activity.

CHAPTER 1

Experiencing/Expressing

The choreographer's work is set in action by an innate urge to create new forms that present the individual's unique response to life's experiences. While one aspect of human nature prompts us to become an integral part of our cultural milieu and preserve our heritage, another aspect urges us to break through the cultural mold so that we may explore new paths and bring our experiences together in new ways. How we develop our creative potential is influenced by our environment and our interaction with it.

Humans are dependent on a constant interchange between the inner and outer world. The taking in from the outer world involves not only basic ingredients, such as air and nutrition, but also sensory input. A constant flow of sensory data (visual, aural, tactile, and kinesthetic) makes possible the experiencing of our world: nature, objects, people, and events. The sensory input sets up an inner stimulation to act. It is through this process of taking in that we enrich our experiencing and through the process of giving out that we give expression to our discoveries. The impulse to explore and create grows out of the ongoing transaction between the inner and the outer worlds.

The constant flow of sensory input from the outer world makes it necessary for us to bring together the elements and fragments of daily encounters—the isolated experiences—into a meaningful

5

relationship. This process leads to symbolization, the ordering of our experiences.

The symbolic transformation of experience is frequently expressed through words, but not always. Sometimes we find that words are completely inadequate to express our response to some of life's encounters, especially the felt aspects of experience. In these instances, we turn to other media, such as motion, sound, or painting, as a means of expression.

Today we recognize that human beings process information in different ways and use different kinds of symbolization as means of expression. Susanne Langer (1942) describes the human potential for two kinds of symbolization: discursive and presentational. The *discursive form* uses words as a means of bringing experience together in a meaningful way. The sequential arrangement of words makes this form linear in structure. The *presentational form of symbolization* is metaphoric in nature and presents the essence of felt thought through the use of imagery and illusion. Choreography would be considered a presentational form of symbolization.

Our potential for creativity and our basic need for form are primary factors that influence the shaping of art forms. The choreographer, like the musician, painter, or sculptor responding to an inner impulse and imaginative thought process, creates a new entity or art form that embodies selected sensory experiences and felt thought.

The Nature of Creativity

How does one describe creativity that plays such a central role in symbolization and expression? Certainly it is not characterized by imitation, conformity, or fitting into preconceived patterns. Creativity implies imaginative thought: sensing, feeling, imaging, and searching for truth. Edmund Sinnott, a biologist, has described creativity as the "organizing power of life" (1959: 26). Alden B. Dow, an architect, defines creativity as the ability "to transform that which is meaningless into a thing of meaning and beauty" (1959: 43). One might ask: How does the process of transforming and organizing, so basic to the creative act, relate to human thought process?

In an effort to better understand the mode of thought that makes possible the flash that results in creative discovery, we often turn to the statements made by artists. Again and again their descriptions of those breakthrough moments when the raw material falls into place suggests that they are functioning in a special state of consciousness. What is the nature of this special state of consciousness associated with the creative act?

Our mode of thought ranges from the highly conscious to the deeply unconscious. When we are functioning at the highly conscious level, we are concerned with the outer world of reality and action. At the deeply unconscious level, our interaction with the outer world is diminished, memory traces are deeply anchored, and there is less interest in action and more concern with self-experience. Between these polarities is believed to be another level of mental activity that has been identified as "pre-conscious" (Kubie, 1942). This mode of thought makes possible the effortless bringing together of fragments and isolated elements of experience into new constellations. Drawing on affective states and sensory imagery, a spontaneous stream of thought results in clustering around a preconceived goal.

Harold Rugg (1963), after years of research, identified this special state of consciousness as the *transliminal mind*, the critical threshold between the conscious and unconscious where creativity takes place. According to Rugg:

> The key to the creative act lies neither in the conscious nor the unconscious. It lies in the threshold antechamber between them. In both the conscious and unconscious the "flash" (imaginative discovery) is definitely censored. The creative act, which depends on freedom, is blocked at both rigid ends of the continuum—the "transliminal mind" is the only part of the continuum that is clearly free from censorship. It is off guard, relaxed, receptive to messages but is also magnetic, with a dynamic forming power (1963: 214, 293).

Transliminally, the organism functions in a condition of relative freedom to create novel forms of image and conception. These forms are not dominated by the deep unconscious or demands of external reality. Yet, in its transliminal functioning, the organism has access to both internal and external resources (Rugg, 1963: 61).

What has been described as the role of the preconscious and the transliminal mind in the creative act is similar to what is thought to be the specialized function of the right hemisphere of the brain. Research related to the hemispheric specialization of the brain (Bogen, 1974; Ornstein, 1974; Sperry, 1969) makes it quite apparent that we have more than one way of processing information—more than one way of thinking. These two processes can be thought of as verbal and nonverbal. We are most familiar with the mental activity of the left hemisphere of the brain, which processes information sequentially, part by part, in an analytical and logical manner. Language is the means of communication for the left/verbal side of the brain. In contrast, the right hemisphere is believed to be more holistic than sequential in handling data. This hemisphere appears to have special ability in identifying shapes, responding to complex wholes and interrelationships. It relies more on imagery than words and is receptive to feeling states. Though each hemisphere is able to function independently and assume a dominant role in specific aspects of the thought process, there is an ever-present, active interrelationship between the two hemispheres that contributes to our total thought process.

What then is the relationship of the hemispheric specializations to the creative activity in choreography? Dance, a nonverbal medium of expression, is certainly dependent on a mode of consciousness that is different from the ordinary mode of thought associated with the left hemisphere. The imaginative thought process in choreography, which involves a spontaneous flow of imagery, the grouping of separate elements, and the holistic forming of the inner vision, would seem to have its roots in the specialized functioning of the right hemisphere of the brain.

However, it is interesting to note recent research suggests that this kind of specific localization may not be valid. Howard Gardener, a neuropsychologist, asserts:

> What remains a complete mystery for a student of neuropsychology are the most comprehensive aspects of artistic production. We can, to be sure, say something about the particular skills involved in artistry. We could even say something about the motivation and the style of artistic work. But as for the overall conception, its sources, its execution, its evaluation—these remain as unilluminated by studies of brain damaged as by studies of normal and talented individuals.
>
> My own guess is that studies of localization of function may well be inappropriate here. To produce something well organized, let alone something fresh and original, it may be necessary to have an essentially intact nervous system (1982: 334).

In his book *Frames of Mind: The Theory of Multiple Intelligences*, Gardner discusses what he believes to be a biological basis for specialized intelligences. He argues that there is persuasive evidence for the existence of several relatively autonomous intellectual competencies that he refers to as "human intelligences." These intelligences are identified as linguistic, musical, logical-mathematical, spatial, bodily-kinesthetic, and personal intelligences. Dance is included in the bodily-kinesthetic intelligence (Gardner, 1983: 8).

There is much that we still do not understand about brain functioning and especially its relationship to the creative act. However, we do know from experience that human beings have a potential for creativity that is given outward form through artistic activity and that this achievement is somehow related to a special state of consciousness. Our task then is to understand what is known about the imaginative thought process and to discover ways of gaining access to the special state of consciousness that makes creativity possible. The question is how to free the innate creative potential and nourish it.

Children find it very natural to respond creatively. Their daily play is filled with imaginative activity. They find great joy in making their own movement patterns, creating new musical sounds, and using their hands to create a painting or clay sculpture. When the imaginative activity and the creative use of movements is so apparent in children's behavior, why doesn't it continue to flower and develop as a child matures into adulthood? No doubt one of the reasons is the increasing influence of outside forces. As a child's world expands and becomes more complex, the expectations of others begin to have greater influence on his or her behavior. Spontaneity and freshness, so apparent in the earlier years, begins to disappear. There is less and less listening to the inner voice and more and more attending to the outer voices. The individual is increasingly pressed to conform to external expectations, and the fear of not being right becomes a powerful force in shaping behavior. As a result, self-directed and creative responses happen less and less.

This statement made by a dance student in one of my workshop classes clearly illustrates how our responses can be shaped and controlled by outside forces:

It is difficult to articulate precisely what occurred in this class in regard to my ability to create and to perform. . . . This method of working is somewhat new to me, but it seems that what has been called for (to work, evolve, develop, grow) has involved not so much what is outside of me but rather what is inside of me. . . . This method insists that one feel (on some emotional level) and act on those feelings, i.e., develop movements.

This is completely antithetical to everything I was ever taught—I was taught not to feel and to be in command of my emotions. Failing that, the next best tact was to disallow these sentiments. Public display of such weaknesses of character was unspeakably dishonorable.

It is not surprising that, even at the fourth class, I still felt inhibited and reticent; to tread lightly is too long with me and too deeply plowed; and here I was being asked to believe that what I feel is valid and to trust in the sincerity and goodwill of the others involved. That I can even dare to commit this to paper must surely attest to what I have achieved in this class.

It can only be presumed that the freeing and discarding of a lifetime of resentment, pain, and anger served to release my inner self to pursue and possibly fulfill my creative potential (Theresa).

This statement does not imply that standards and expectations have no place in our lives. Of course they do play an important role in human development. However, these external forces should be experienced in such a way that they do not stifle our creative development. The creative potential of each person should be valued and nurtured through a variety of self-directed activities in an environment that is supportive and nonjudgmental.

Developing a Creative Environment for Dance Classes

If we are to be successful in developing our potential as fully functioning individuals, we must be concerned with nurturing both the inner and outer ways of experiencing and expressing. We must not only make it possible for individuals to find a comfortable fit within the cultural mold, but also to break through the mold in order to make imaginative discoveries and enrich themselves and their culture. The teacher of choreography is faced with important questions: How do you create an atmosphere that encourages students to attend inwardly and become aware of feelings and images? How do you free students so that they are able to allow the inner voice to guide the flow of movement and the shaping of the externalized movement event? In other words, how do you create an environment that makes it possible for the individual to respond intuitively and let the movement form autonomously?

Freedom and Trust

Fear and lack of trust are important factors that have a profound effect on our ability to act creatively. The feeling of fear, arising out of concern about being right and meeting the expectations of others, blocks our ability to respond intuitively. Lack of trust, in ourselves and in the environment, makes it difficult, if not impossible, to be open to the experience and allow the inner impulse to guide the movement event. Only when we feel a sense of freedom and trust in the learning environment is it possible to take risks and make a unique statement. Once we are free to take risks and to be vulnerable, each new experience and small success builds our self-confidence and a willingness to be involved more fully.

An environment that is sensed as psychologically safe is dependent on three major conditions: evaluation that is self-directed, relaxation of body and mind, and a structural design that is developmentally oriented.

Nonjudgmental Climate

Undoubtedly the first and most basic requirement for a dance situation designed to nurture creativity is the establishment of a nonjudgmental environment, in which individuals feel free to respond intuitively without the threat of having their creative efforts judged as right or wrong. Such a place makes it possible for dancers to trust the situation and learn to trust themselves.

Most students who enter a choreography class expect the teacher to assign problem-solving studies that will be presented and then discussed by teacher and class in relation to the assigned task. Though the intent of this approach is to help students learn, my experience suggests that this kind of learning environment tends to block rather than free students to develop creatively. They find themselves caught between listening to their own inner voices and the expectations of external voices (i.e., the assignment given by the teacher). As a result, the creative work often seems contrived and lacking in authenticity.

A major role of the teacher is to free students so that they can discover and develop their innate resources. Rather than acting as judge or evaluator, the teacher's role should be first to facilitate experiences that help students discover their potential to feel, image, and respond intuitively. In other words, establish a learning environment where what is possible for the individual can actually happen. Secondly, the teacher's task is to help students become confident and proficient in self-observation and inner-oriented

evaluation. A nonjudgmental environment plays a significant role in making possible this kind of experiencing and evaluating.

Structural Design

A significant factor in the establishment of an environment that is sensed as psychologically safe is the overall design of experiences. Before plunging students into creating dance studies, there should be many opportunities for them to explore various aspects of the process through self-directed activities that are sensitively guided by the teacher. The early experiences should assist the students in getting in touch with inner sensations, feelings, and images, and becoming aware of the aesthetic elements inherent in movement: energy, space, and rhythm. These experiences should be planned so that they assist the students in progressing successfully from one developmental stage to the next. After a foundation is established, there should be opportunity for students to start creating dance studies using their own motivation. Experiential work will be greatly enriched by discussions that contribute to an increased understanding of creativity and the art process.

There are many threads of experience, each of which must be approached developmentally and, at the same time, these various threads must be interwoven in such a way that they become a tapestry—an organic whole. Sensitively planned and guided experiences contribute immensely to the student's sense of security and trust.

Process

The journey from the choreographer's intent and inner vision to the finished dance form is guided by an inner process. André Malraux (1953) has described this process as "seeing, reducing, and forming." But what are the specific aspects of the process that bring about seeing, reducing, and forming? What is happening in the internal process that results in the final form? How does this apply to choreography?

Sometimes the choreographer starts work with a definite intent or image, other times the motivation is vague so that there is a period of exploration before the inner vision becomes clear. Regardless of the way the choreographer works, the fundamental nature of the process is the same. According to Harold Rugg, "the complete act of expression has three major phases: deep feeling, a long looking and absorbing, preparing, gathering of self and the task; a period of perception in-depth, cutting through and under conventional ways of seeing . . . finally putting down what the artist sees, striving to make his statement equivalent to his created forms of feeling" (1963: 31).

How are these three major phases of the creative act translated into specific experiences that contribute to our creative growth? First, there must be an understanding of the nature of the process and its basic components: sensing, feeling, imaging, transforming, and forming. These components provide a functional framework for the choreographic experience. Each component should be experienced in depth so that its relationship to the total process is understood. Then the various components can become functional in the overall organic forming process.

These various phases of the creative process might be described in the following way:

Sensing

- Learns to see, absorb, and perceive in depth.
- Becomes aware of inner sensations associated with sensory input.

Feeling

- Gets in touch with feelings associated with life's encounters—becoming aware of bodily sensations.

Imaging

- Gains access to our capacity to recall images and create new ones.
- Frees our thought processes so that images can emerge, unfold, and shift in a kaleidoscopic fashion.

- Uses images and imagination as a means of discovery.

Transforming

- Discovers the aesthetic qualities that are integrally related to the images and evolving felt thought.
- Allows the felt thought that emerges from the sense data and images to be transformed into movement ideas that go beyond the original experience.

Forming

- Allows movement ideas to take shape organically.
- Integrates the aesthetic elements in such a way that the final dance form creates the desired illusion and presents metaphorically the inner vision.

The Creative Process

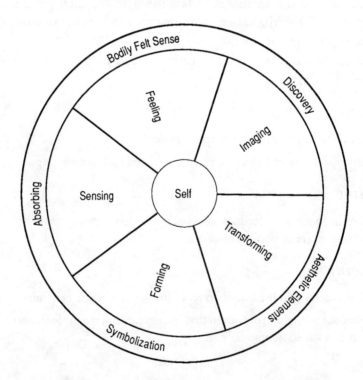

The preceding diagram presents a structural framework for the choreographic experience. It illustrates the flow and interrelatedness of the various phases of the process. Though the creative act may start with sensing and end with forming, there is an ongoing interplay between the different phases throughout the process.

The choreographer, who is deeply involved in creating, often moves back and forth between the motivation and the envisioned final form. Though the focus may shift according to the needs of the choreographer, the process is experienced as a whole and not as a linear happening.

As Iredell Jenkins has so aptly stated:

> Creation, the culmination of this process, is most exactly conceived as vibrating between two poles. . . . It looks backward toward its source seeking to attain a clear apprehension of the particularity it is dealing with. At the same time, it looks forward toward its product, seeking through this to make its vision more articulate and permanent. These two phases can be described as internalization and externalization or as insight and embodiment or as contemplation and concretion. The important point is that these are phases in a cycle that is cohesive and recurrent. . . . The creative cycle and so the whole process comes to a climax when these phases are fused into a single entity; this is the vision of the artist become concrete and given to us through his work of art as embodied insight (1958: 117).

Creating involves an autonomous act that is holistic in nature. Each phase of the process plays an important role but always in relationship to the whole. In the following chapters each component—seeing, feeling, imaging, transforming, and forming—will be discussed in relation to the choreographic process. Sample movement experiences will be described illustrating ways of facilitating learning in each area. The emphasis throughout is on the early experiences that provide a foundation for the choreographic process. Though I have found these experiences to be effective in helping individuals discover and understand the various components of the process, they are not intended as a set formula. They are included as examples that illustrate a way of working. You must find your own approach to images and movement tasks that assist in the discovery of movement as a means of expression.

CHAPTER 2

Seeing

"Seeing is not such an easy thing as it is supposed to be."
—Robert Henri

People, especially adults, are expected to see clearly and fully. But do they? Seeing for some of us is limited to the general impression of that which is observed, whether it is nature, persons, objects, or events. In our rush, we dash from object to object, event to event, with little awareness of detail or the aesthetic qualities of that which is encountered. We look but we do not see.

Most of us are able to name, identify, and categorize that which we observe. Of course, the ability to recognize and classify does contribute to our everyday functioning and therefore is important. But is this limited kind of seeing and sensing enough? If we are interested in creativity and its development, then the answer must be no.

Seeing is a primary source of sensory data that sparks the imaginative process. Any individual who is working creatively is not concerned so much with labeling as becoming aware of the form and spatial relationships, the inner structure as well as the outer shape of an object, and in sensing the qualities that pervade the experience. The creative person is able to turn toward an encounter

with openness and become deeply absorbed in the specific experience. It is as though the observer becomes one with that which
is being observed. During this period of attending, we are able to
see each in our own unique way—seeing what is important at the
moment.

This intense kind of seeing is illustrated by Georgia O'Keeffe's
description of an observation that provided the stimulus for one of
her earlier paintings:

> I walked up Riverside Drive with two or three other students . . . we
> sat down on the grass. When I looked about at the night I saw two
> tall poplar trees breathing—rustling in the light spring air. The
> foliage was thick and dark and soft—the grass bright with moon-
> light. The river, near—with the twinkling lights from the other side,
> far away. I studied the outline of the trees carefully. The openings
> where the sky came through—the unevenness of the edges—the
> mass of trees, dark, solid, very alive. Next morning I tried to paint
> it (1976: xii).

This same sensitivity and ability to see in detail is revealed in her
description of a juniper weed that was the inspiration of another
painting:

> It is a beautiful white trumpet flower with strong veins that hold the
> flower open and grow longer than the round part of the flower—
> twisting as they grow off beyond it. In the tropics where the plant
> grows almost to the size of a small tree these ribs sometimes curl an
> inch and a half beyond the flowers and the blossoms droop instead
> of looking up at you. Some of them are a pale green in the center—
> some are a pale Mars velvet (1976: 84).

Ansel Adams' account of his experience with the painter John
Marin illustrates Marin's ability to become deeply absorbed in that
which he encountered:

> Marin would spend days wandering about in the Taos country,
> sometimes painting, but mostly looking about, watching cloud
> formations and just sitting on a rock waiting for something to
> happen. He stored impressions in his mind and when the creative
> pressures asserted themselves, he would work almost feverishly for

hours, completing one water color after another with enormous energy and concentration. Then after the production cycle was over he would return to a passive, soaking up period. Marin would make statements such as "I am always exploring something—a rock, a tree, a face, or a cloud—the more I look the more I see" (1985: 309).

Ansel Adams' descriptions of his own work as a photographer point out the central role that seeing—observing—plays in the art process:

> It is increasingly clear to me that my art relates more and more to sublimation of my closeness to the natural world, its events, light itself, and the positive. What I do seems natural and simple to me; to others it may appear as miraculous performance. It is neither simple nor miraculous; it is a personal expression based on observation and reaction that I am not able to define except in terms of the work itself (1985: 339).

Statements such as these illustrate the way creative people are able to see and respond to their environment. As Rollo May has said, "the essence of art is a powerful and alive encounter between the artist and his world" (1975: 52).

Using Observation to Teach Creative Movement

It is possible to help individuals learn to see more fully and become more aware of their environment. While I was teaching an experimental class in choreography, I decided to try using specific observations as a means of helping students increase their ability to see. I started by asking them to observe a vine—any vine. I suggested that they look at the vine as though they had never seen it before and to return to it several times during the week. As a guide I suggested questions such as these: What do you see? How does it feel? What qualities do you sense? What are its movement characteristics?

At the beginning of the next session, we shared our observations—what we had seen. As the students described what they had observed, it became apparent that different people experienced in different ways, but running through all the comments about the vine was a feeling of clinging and thrusting, sometimes giving a sense of holding or choking, and other times reaching out and expanding. Some students experienced qualities that were strong while others sensed delicate qualities. As we shared what we had seen and felt, we became aware of how the experience had been different for each student, and this awareness stimulated us to see and sense more deeply.

Later in the experiential part of the class, students had an opportunity to transform what they had seen and felt into movement studies. This process involved having a clear image, attending to qualities, and finally letting the inner-sensing provide the impulse for the externalized movement: Let the movement happen.

In most instances, the dance studies growing out of this type of observation reflect feelings and aesthetic qualities associated with observation. But occasionally an individual may find that the movement response motivated by the sensory experience triggers images that are related to personal experience. One student described the imagery that emerged from her movement response to a vine in this way:

> My vine became my relationship pattern—one of totally giving up? I gave up because that is the way I perceive relationships of commitment to be. It's wrong. My movement showed me what I feel inside myself. Why can't I feel without the movement? (Karen)

In instances like this, the externalized movement event embodies personal meaning as well as aesthetic qualities.

In the following weeks, we continued the observations using a variety of subjects: different aspects of nature, objects, and living forms. In each instance, suggestions were offered to provide a focus for the observation.

As we progressed, I would suggest that the students determine what they believe to be the dominant and less dominant characteristics of the observed objects. As we discussed their observations,

I would include visual material from other arts and quotes from artists that were relevant to our discussion.

During the movement session, there was opportunity for improvisation based on their observation. The following exercises illustrate the way observations may be presented.

Machines

- Observe different machines: in the workplace; on the street; in the home.
- Attend to the motion and rhythmic characteristics of the machine.
- Sense the qualities inherent in its action.
- Select one machine to study.
- Become aware of its unique characteristics: motion; rhythmic pattern; and underlying qualities.

Birds

- Observe different kinds of birds in motion: hummingbird; seagull; hawk; peacock.
- Be aware of their flight patterns: fast; slow; floating; soaring; darting.
- What qualities do you sense in their action: strong; delicate; smooth; sharp; vibrating?
- Do you feel a contrast in their use of energy?
- Select one bird. Study its movement characteristics and the qualities revealed in its action.

Buildings

- Observe different buildings in your community: homes; business structures; museums; churches.
- Attend to the overall shape of the building.
- Be aware of the use of repetition.
- What about contrast? How is it used?
- What gives the building a feeling of unity?

- Select one building and study it carefully.

Trees

- Observe different kinds of trees: oak; willow; palm; evergreen; sycamore.
- What do you sense as the overall feeling of the trees?
- What about the texture?
- What is the spatial pattern, lines, and relationships?
- What qualities do you sense: delicate; strong; bold?
- Select one tree and observe it carefully. Determine what you sense as the dominant characteristic and the less dominant features.

The ongoing observations and discussions revealed that students were seeing—experiencing specific encounters—with increased sensitivity and greater awareness. This new awareness of sensory data enriched their creative work. Increased ability to see beneath the surface and to become aware of specific elements, relationships, and underlying qualities of an object or event helped them in working imaginatively from their own motivation. Increased sensitivity provided the inner impulse to respond spontaneously and explore movement possibilities.

What were the students' reactions to this aspect of the experience? The following excerpts taken from their written personal reflections reveal the ways that they sensed their achievements:

It was wonderful to feel how alert my vision became [during] those weeks that we had visual tasks (observations). And how rich experience became when I shared what I noticed with others and heard their perceptions (Gayle).

I feel as if so much has happened in such a short time—the early discussions about functioning more in the right brain mode have enlightened me to the extraordinary beauty of the external world. Rather than intellectually labeling things, I am learning to allow myself to experience them through my senses. I am learning to truly perceive. Even the simplest thing is radiating with sensory stimuli. I feel reborn to my senses as if I had been blind, deaf, and dumb all of my life (Sam).

As I reflect back over my experience I feel that a lot of growth and learning has taken place for me—I have felt a real sense of freedom in my life, both a freedom in movement and in my thought process which seems to be broadening. It is as if things around me have taken on a fresh meaning or a deeper more significant dimension. For example, when I am out walking or running all the beauty of nature seems to mean so much more to me.

The experience of observing machines and other aspects of the city environment proved to be very helpful. First, I had to break down my resistance to addressing these subjects. I would much rather deal with nature. Second, I had to view these through different eyes, seeing qualities and elements rather than just having a negative emotional response—today I feel much more a part of life around me (Jenny).

Becoming more perceptive and able to see detail, relationships, and form not only enriches our lives and stimulates creative responses, but also serves a very practical role in responding to the creative work of other artists and in assessing the result of our own creative work. For example, when video recording and playback is used as a means of self-evaluation of choreography, the student is able to see the inner structure of the work—elements, relationships, dynamics, continuity, unity—and determine whether the movement development enhances or interferes with the objectification of his or her inner vision.

Summary

Seeing and sensing are basic ingredients in the creative act. The sensory input provides the stimulus and raw material that is imaginatively transformed and given external form. Therefore, it is important that the choreographer be able to respond to personal encounters with a high degree of sensitivity and to see/perceive the essence and qualitative aspects of life experiences that are basic to artistic activity.

CHAPTER 3

Feeling

Our interactions with the surrounding world, nature, objects, people, and situations are accompanied by feelings. But often our awareness of these inner sensations or feelings remains vague and unclear. We may even try to deny or ignore them, especially if they seem negative or disturbing. Our culture tends to devalue the felt dimensions of life's experiences even though feelings are an integral aspect of the human response. This is unfortunate, because in so doing we are cutting off an important element that affects the functioning of the total organism. Instead of ignoring or blocking our feelings we need to respect them, become skilled at getting in touch with them, and allow feelings to participate in the process of clarifying experience and giving it meaningful form. We must not only know how to interact with the external world in a logical and analytical way, we must also know how to get in touch with the inner world and to nurture our intuitive-imaginative response.

Artists know very well that feelings are basic ingredients in the creative process. Ben Shahn, in his discussion of the artist and his work, states:

> [The artist] must never fail to be involved in the pleasures and
> desperations of mankind, for in them lies the very source of feeling
> upon which the work of art is registered; the work of art is a creative
> image and the symbol of a specific value; it was made to contain

permanently something that was felt and thought, and believed. It contains that feeling and nothing else (1957: 93, 123).

Aaron Copland, the composer, speaking about the background of his creative work, writes:

What, after all do I put down when I put down notes? I put down a reflection of emotional states; feelings, perceptions, imaginings, intuitions. An emotional state, as I use the term, is compounded of everything we are: our background, our environment, our convictions. Art particularizes and makes actual these fluent emotional states. Because it particularizes and makes it actual, it gives meaning to "la condition humaine" (1959: 117).

Anna Sokolow, in writing about her approach to choreography, states: "Movements are not intellectually contrived but are evoked by emotional images. . . *Rooms* was choreographed without music. I wanted to do something about people in a big city. The theme loneliness and noncommunication evolved as I worked. . . . In *Opus 58,* I wanted the feeling of a new era, one where life is violent, precarious, and the individual seems unimportant" (1965: 33, 36).

Susanne Langer, the philosopher, writing about the role of feeling in art, states: "that what language does not readily do—present the nature and patterns of sensitive and emotive life—is done by works of art. Such works are expressive forms and what they express is the nature of human feeling." Then, relating this idea to dance, she writes: "What is the work of art for—the dance, the virtual dynamic image? To express its creator's ideas of immediate, felt emotive life. To set forth directly what feeling is like. A dance is not a symptom of a dancer's feeling, but an expression of its composer's knowledge of many feelings" (1957: 8).

The role of feeling becomes apparent when we recall some of the magical moments we have experienced during a dance concert. In those instances, something more than a visual experience was happening. Our sensing and overall awareness was not so much concerned with the technical performance or the theatrical effects as with the energy flow, the vitality of the event, and above all the inner substance of the work. We found ourselves being drawn in, participating vicariously, and deeply absorbed in the unfolding of the movement event. Our involvement in the creative work called forth a deep inner-sensing at the felt level and stimulated our imagination. In order for a piece of choreography to have the power to evoke this kind of aesthetic response, it must emanate from a deep inner-sensing and reflect a constant interplay between the internal felt sense and the externalized movement.

The choreographer's task then is to become aware of the felt dimension of experience and images that set a new work in progress. This inner-oriented process requires that you temporarily separate yourself from the external world and in a state of relaxed concentration attend inwardly. From this inner listening comes an awareness and impulse for the externalization of felt thought in a form that we know as dance.

Some form of relaxation is helpful in cutting off the impinging external stimuli and shifting the focus to inner-sensing. I find that the method known as progressive relaxation (see the Appendix for a description) is effective for several reasons. The focus is on sensing in the muscles, becoming aware of tension signals, and then releasing tension. As one reduces the residual tension held in the muscles, the ability to attend inwardly is enhanced. The state of relaxed concentration with emphasis on inner-sensing helps one get in touch with feelings and gain access to the intuitive mode of consciousness. In this special state of consciousness, feelings and the unfolding images spark the impulse that leads to the externalization of the inner experiencing. The following statement describes one person's experience with relaxation:

> The relaxation helped me tremendously to get in touch with my body and allowing it to take whatever direction it wanted to take. I remember being so surprised at the way the body could explore on its own (Mary).

The freeing of the body-mind is an essential aspect of the discovery process and the autonomous forming of the dance event.

When choreography evolves from felt experiences, it reflects the creator's encounter with life, and the interaction between self and world. The resulting form will be perceived as more than an imitation or manipulation of movement. It will possess an inherent integrity and convey a sense of authenticity.

The following statements made by students describe their inner experiences as they relate to choreography:

> The creative process that I am discovering is really there inside of me. It needs to be nurtured, given time, and worked at again and again. The class has given me the freedom to create without someone's judgment upon it, without someone's standard of technique forced upon it, no pressure from old scripts in my mind. My movement can be as free as I want it. I'm neither locked into technique or kept away from it. However in pursuing the purer movements of my imagination, I find myself removed from the technique as I have known it.
>
> It is interesting how my body seems to gravitate towards movements that move into one another. If I am looking for a movement sometimes they will fall into place like a puzzle if I allow them to. They do it by themselves and before I realize it my body has created a movement I like, without my mind involved so to speak. However I have had to put my mind in the right frame of mind to receive (June).

> In this class, I have come to witness my thinking not so much in terms of words but in imagery and feeling—my motivation always springs from my inner feelings. It is this inner feeling which elicits the many images within me. Although these inner motion pictures are often fragmentary, through them I am able to be aware of the intangible feeling within me.
>
> I used to follow my feeling only in making my early draft of choreography. As I continue to get more in tune with my feeling I begin to see images more clearly. It seems that my feeling is multi-dimensional and so are the derived images. I am actually selecting and making connections between the many different images. There seems to be a flow or logic behind the process—it is not verbal thinking but thinking in terms of feeling. For me feeling is thought too (Donald).

Motivating Dance Movement Based on Feelings

Movement events that grow out of feelings and inner-sensing do not happen all at once nor do they arrive in full bloom. Learning to work at a deep level of involvement takes time. We are so accustomed to judging our outward expression that often in the middle of the process we begin thinking "this is not good" or "I should try something different." When we interrupt the process and respond in that way, we are shifting away from the basic state of relaxed concentration to the outer- oriented mode of thought. This frustrates our feeling of being involved. Involvement requires that we attend inwardly to the bodily felt sense and then allow the impulse for externalized movement to evolve from the inner sensation. Young choreographers must have many opportunities to discover and develop their ability to function at a deep level of involvement and to transform the felt experience into aesthetic forms.

Usually the first movement responses that are truly involved are of short duration. I call these early externalized movement events "fragments." For the first time the student is able to let it happen. The movement starts and then suddenly ends. But when movement begins to unfold and my eyes tell me that this is authentic movement flowing from inner-sensing, I know that an important accomplishment is in process. For in that moment, the movement output and inner-sensing are in harmony. The organism is functioning as an integrated whole. I know that with more experience and time, these fragments will grow into movement patterns of longer duration and finally into complex forms. When choreography grows out of this kind of involvement, it will embody the authentic statement of the choreographer and have the power to evoke an aesthetic response in the audience.

What is the nature of the learning environment that makes it possible for young choreographers to develop their potential for inner-sensing and responding to their feelings? What kind of movement tasks, or experiences, will enable them to be involved at the felt level and to let movement happen spontaneously? Allowing movement triggered by feelings to flow spontaneously is usually a new and often frightening experience for many people. After pondering these questions at some length and then exploring different approaches, I found that the use of images and selected word cues were not only effective but a powerful means of getting in touch with feelings and allowing them to provide the impulse for the movement response.

Obviously the first tasks must be simple and psychologically safe. This phase, like so many other aspects of creative work, must be approached developmentally. I have found that the early movement responses that reflect involvement at the felt level usually happen at a very basic and personal level. Learning to transcend the immediate felt experience to allow the intuitive process to select and imaginatively shape the essence of experience into aesthetic forms that are more abstract and universal in nature takes time. You should not be surprised to discover the early creative output happening at a very personal level. When you are in the beginning stages of exploring how to get in touch with your feelings, how could it be otherwise? Inexperienced choreographers need experiences that open the way and gradually nudge them into seeing in new ways eventually transcending the specific encounter and feelings that set the work in progress.

Some images are more effective than others in evoking movement responses. I have found the following three guidelines useful in selecting appropriate images. First, images should lend themselves to an action response, or movement that flows from the bodily felt sense. Secondly, images should be open-ended and allow for a spontaneous self-directed response. Thirdly, images should provide progression from concrete images that are readily available and psychologically safe to abstract images that draw on personal experiences and are more symbolic in nature.

In the following exercises, the hoop and elastic band are concrete images that could be used early on to stimulate inner-sensing. They are outer-oriented and focus on a one-to-one relationship with something external. The image of concealing and revealing is not as specific and requires a more introspective response that draws from various personal encounters and felt responses. The abstract image has the potential to evoke a movement response that develops and takes its own shape.

Concrete Images

Hoop

- Sitting in a comfortable position with your eyes closed, imagine a straight line passing down through the center of your head, the center of your torso, and into the floor. Trace a straight line again, like a pole, down through the head, torso, and into the floor.

- Now have the image that you are sitting inside a hoop that is resting on the floor. I don't know its size, or how far away from your body it is. Have a clear image of the hoop that is surrounding you.

- Keeping your center line very straight, lean slowly toward the edge of the hoop. Lean in any direction but be aware of your center as you move outward. Then slowly return to the starting position. Repeat the leaning toward the edge but always return to center.

- Explore leaning in different directions and sense the relationship of your center to the hoop.

  Comment. The hoop is a familiar object that defines a boundary and is sensed as safe. Attending to the center line not only heightens inner-sensing but also increases awareness of one's center. Exploration of leaning is self-directed. Moving the center in relationship to the hoop increases awareness of the spatial factor.

Elastic Band

- Sit in a comfortable position. Have the image of a rather light elastic band. Hold one end in each hand.

- Now begin to stretch the elastic in any direction, but keep it close to the body. See how many ways you can stretch the band and release it. Allow time for exploration.

• Now begin to pull farther from the body out into space. Stretch the band in different directions. Continue to explore on your own in different directions.

• Now have a feeling that the elastic band is very strong; explore pulling it in different directions.

• Let the movement take you to your knees and feet, but take your time. Let it develop.

Comment. An elastic band is a concrete object, and stretching is a familiar experience. The emphasis is on awareness and the inner-sensing of the pull. The action is a self-directed movement. This simple experience allows the student to become involved in a safe situation. Taking the movement to the knees and feet requires considerable involvement. Observation of each student's response reveals very clearly whether the movement is coming from a felt involvement or a mechanical response. If the involvement cannot be sustained, the movement should be continued, in a sitting position.

Abstract Images

An abstract image, in contrast to a concrete one, is more passive in nature and involves a surrendering, or letting go. The openness of the abstract image provides a freedom that allows students to draw on feelings associated with personal experiences. The focus of attention is on the inner world. The following examples illustrate how an abstract image may be presented.

Something You Don't Like

• In a comfortable sitting position, have an image of something that you don't like. It may be over your head, on your shoulders or back. It is pushing you down.

• Be clear about the image. Where do you feel it? Make contact with it. Try to get rid of it.

• Let it move on its own.

Comment. This image will usually evoke the memory of an experience about which the dancer will have strong personal feelings. Though this very personal response is not the ultimate goal in dance, it does help the students to discover inner-sensing associated with feeling.

Concealing—Sometimes Revealing

- Sit with arms wrapped tightly around the torso. Let one elbow attempt to move outward into space, then return.

- Continue exploring with either elbow but always return to the tightly held position. Allow time for exploration.

- Hold for a minute, but keep your concentration.

- Now have the image of a person concealing but sometimes trying to reveal. Concentrate on the image and the feelings.

- Then let the movement happen: concealing but sometimes revealing. Allow time for development.

Comment. This illustrates how one can use a movement preparation so that the transition to the image is made smoothly. The opening and closing of the held position initiates an inner-sensing that is easily extended to the image of concealing and revealing. I find that the preparation is a significant factor in the success of the image.

Carefully selected word cues can be an effective means of getting in touch with the bodily felt sense. The words, to be effective, must have potential to evoke inner-sensing as well as action. Words such as *darting, quivering, twisting,* and *dangling* are useful. For example: "Have a sense of dangling. Let it move, shift in any way but keep the feeling of dangling."

Tightening and Loosening

Word cues can be useful in stimulating responses that are in contrast or opposition. For example, tightening and loosening:

- In a standing position, explore the feeling of tightening in the whole body.

- Then shift to the feeling of loosening.

- Then continue going between tightening and loosening in different ways.

- Then let the movement develop in any direction, either staying in one place or moving about.

Comment. In this kind of experience timing is important. First, the individual must become involved and attend to inner-sensing. Then, spontaneous movement exploration of tightening and loosening can begin. The teacher's eyes must become trained in sensing when to shift activity. Experiencing contrasting cues, such as tightening and loosening, gives a sense of potential polarities in movement qualities. The kinesthetic discovery of the possible range in movement qualities is fundamental to creative work.

Summary

The discovery and imaginative use of feelings requires:

1. Giving of self to an encounter, being receptive, becoming absorbed, and learning to see and feel in depth.

2. Becoming aware of feelings, bodily felt sense, and images that emerge from an encounter with our world.

3. Experiencing a freedom that allows the transformation of the bodily felt sense and inner vision into movement qualities that are given form through the movement event.

Creative work can be facilitated through the use of well-chosen images and selected word cues. The early experiences that involve the bodily felt sense may be approached through the use of images that bring one in touch with kinesthetic awareness (sensing in the muscles). These kinesthetic experiences provide a foundation for abstract images that draw on personal encounters and the associated feelings and images. Abstract images, carefully selected and presented, have the potential to evoke a wide range of imaginative responses. These provide the foundation for the imaginative discovery and inner vision that takes shape as a dance form.

CHAPTER 4

Imaging

Imagination, acting as an instrument of discovery, propels the creative thought process toward the objectification of inner-sensed images and feelings. In the case of choreography, the inner discovery is presented metaphorically through a newly created dance form. This means that images and felt experiences are transformed into movement elements and qualities in such a way that the movement event presents an objectification of inner experiencing.

The unfolding event is fueled by an interplay between the inner-outer happenings, a kind of feed forward/feedback process. The original stimulus sets in action images and feelings that are transformed into kinetic energy and then released spontaneously through movement.

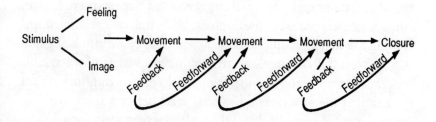

This objectification through externalized movement provides an immediate feedback to the organism and sparks a new flow of feelings and images that are again externalized through movement. This inner-outer process continues until the metaphoric statement finds closure. The unfolding process that emerges from the inner response and outer objectification provides a resonating and driving force that gives a sense of aliveness and authenticity to the ongoing dance event.

In order for a new synthesis or dance form to emerge from this feed forward/feedback process, the choreographer must be actively engaged in the imaginative thought process. One must sustain concentration, attend to inner-sensing and emerging images, then let the movement happen spontaneously. It is the ability to imagine that enables the choreographer to view specific experiences and relationships of self to the outside world in new and meaningful ways.

Images, both memory images and newly imagined ones, are basic ingredients in the creative process. They feed the process and play a significant role in bringing about innovative connections between bits of sensory data. The emergent synthesis from this process provides the germinal material for choreography. Memory images range from those associated with sensory input from recent happenings—such as looking at an object, then closing the eyes and seeing a replica of the object—to images related to earlier experiences, which may be buried in the unconscious.

When one is involved in the creative process, images of both recent and past experiences can emerge with amazing speed. Images come together, coalesce, break apart, and find new relationships. During this kaleidoscopic activity, new images come into being and they too can shift, change, and recombine in a variety of ways. This process of coming together, shifting, and reorganizing may go on for a short time or a long time, even years before a final synthesis takes shape. When the breakthrough does happen, one senses immediately that the newly discovered synthesis is right. This moment is often referred to as the "aha" stage. The significant discovery (aha stage) happens when one is functioning in a special state of consciousness. In this non-ordinary mode of thought, one has easy access to a stream of sensory data from the conscious and the unconscious. The mind is off-guard, relaxed, and receptive. One has little sense of time and no awareness of the inner critic. Images flow, scanning happens swiftly, and new constellations are shaped and reshaped.

So the total creative act involves both the non-ordinary and ordinary modes of consciousness. The non-ordinary mode is actively involved in the imaginative and intuitive process: the production of imagery, germinal material, and the autonomous forming process. The ordinary mode plays a dominant role in the early preparation, the sensing and absorbing, and in the later stage when the creator looks with a critical eye at what has emerged from the imaginative process. This assessment may lead to further refinement or to a return to the inner process for new developments.

As one thinks about the brain functioning in relation to dance, it is interesting to note the way Murray Louis described to me his experience during the creative process:

> An inner voice directs and guides me. I will repeat what it says and from this process a form emerges. It happens so fast that I must go back over it in order to know what I have done. Afterwards I step back and view it. Then I will edit, mold, and flesh it out.

His statement implies the involvement of different modes of consciousness. First there is the imaginative thought process and the spontaneous forming of movement set in action by inner experiencing: felt sense and imagery. Then, secondly comes the viewing and final shaping of what was formed autonomously.

Other artists, describing the creative process as they experience it, reveal the crucial role the imagination plays in the creative process. Sculptor Henry Moore tells how imagination is at the heart of true creation:

> Sometimes I start with a set subject—or a sculptural problem I have given myself, and then consciously attempt to build an ordered

relationship of forms, which shall express my idea. But if the work is to be more than a sculptural exercise, unexplainable jumps in the process of thought occur; and imagination plays its part (Ghiselin, 1952: 77).

Painter Ben Shahn describes the give-and-take between imagination and the final product:

From the moment at which a painter begins to strike figures of color upon a surface he must become acutely sensitive to feel, the textures, the light, the relationships which arise before him. At one point he will mold the material according to an intention. At another he may yield to intuition—perhaps a whole concept—to emerging forms, to new implications within the paintings surface. Idea itself—ideas, many ideas move back and forth across his mind as a constant traffic, dominated perhaps by larger currents and directions, by what he wants to think. Thus idea rises to the surface, grows, changes as a painting grows and develops. So one must say that painting is both creative and responsive. It is an intimately communicative affair between the painter and his painting, a conversation back and forth, the painting telling the painter even as it receives its shape and form (1957: 57).

Knowing something about the nature of the imaginative process is one thing, but inspiring an imaginative response is quite another matter. What kind of experiences will help young choreographers discover their potential for responding imaginatively? How does one learn to attend to internal responses to sensory data and allow imagery to form spontaneously? In other words, how does a choreographer become deeply absorbed in the imaginative-intuitive process?

Traditionally the problem-solving method has been used as an approach to choreography. Students are asked to create studies that make use of a specific aspect of composition. A verbal explanation is made, a work period follows, and then the studies are shown. The discussion that follows is concerned with the students' success or lack of success in meeting the specific assignment.

Though this approach may be very useful during certain phases of advanced study, I believe that it is not the most effective way to facilitate creative work during the early stages of development. When the focus is on problem solving, the students' tendency is to use the ordinary thought process and to be concerned about meeting the expectations of the teacher.

If not problem solving, then what? Earlier I discussed the use of imagery as a means of getting in touch with feelings. Here again I find images an excellent means of evoking an authentic movement response.

Relaxation

Some form of relaxation is valuable as preparation for imagery experiences. It reduces external stimuli, helps one gain access to the special mode of consciousness, and inspires the imagination (see Appendix for a description of progressive relaxation). It is in this relaxed state of mind that one is able to let new entities come into being. It is interesting to note students' comments about the role of relaxation.

> Imaging was induced by relaxation. Relaxing and releasing seem to be the key. The more I was able to clear out the external variables, the more I was able to differentiate the clouds from my main objectives. The truer the imagery, the stronger the intensity.
>
> The visualization on the imagined balance beam was when I clicked. I had new knowledge of my center. My motivation was strong and true. I had just turned twenty years of age—young womanhood. I needed to leave my teen years in my back pocket. At first the movement on the imagined balance beam was clumsy. With a new image in mind I became stronger and more self-reliant. A reflection of all the past taught me gave me agility on the balance beam—the acceptance of womanhood (Constance).

> It is in the relaxed state of mind that we learn to let our grasping mind go. We have to drop our preconceived ideas so that we can let new experiences happen (Irving).

However, developing skill in relaxation and being able to sustain a relaxed concentration so basic to creativity takes time. Some students may have difficulty learning to shift attention to internal sensing that requires letting go of external control and opening themselves to new images and ideas. As Rollo May says, "Imagination is the casting off of mooring ropes and taking one's chances that there will be new posts in the vastness beyond" (1975: 120).

Though the imaginative process may be a new and sometimes threatening experience for some individuals, they will soon discover their potential for imaging and the satisfaction that comes from exploring the imaginative thought process. One student's journal describes her discovery of the non-ordinary mode of consciousness:

> I loved having a chance to go inside and use a part of my mind that is completely nonintellectual. I found that part to be full of colors, images, and sensations quite different from normal consciousness. Also as the semester went on, it got easier to go to that part and each time it seemed to get a little deeper. In order for me to get there I had to really relax and let go of my intellect. Sometimes this was a challenge, but if I stuck it out, it was always worth it. I felt like a door opened and all kinds of stored up images and thoughts came spilling out.
>
> The motivation that I chose to work with would vary slightly but it maintained the same theme. The theme had to do with transitions, moving on, and at the same time leaving something behind. One week it was focused on the transition of going from a girl to woman, and what the differences and similarities are. That really clicked and for the first time I really felt something happening with movement. I felt taken over by it as if it was moving me. It also made me realize the difference between when it kind of works and when I really let go and let it take me.
>
> Each week I found it easier and easier to go into the creative part of my mind. It became almost like a switch that could be turned on (Susan).

The Developmental Use of Imagery

The use of imagery as a way of tapping into the intuitive mode of consciousness requires careful selection and presentation. Not all images are effective, and the order in which they are presented makes a difference in the way students are able to open up and take hold; developmental consideration is important.

The aim is to use the image as a starting point, a stimulus that sets the student's imagination in action and provides the impulse for the unfolding of the externalized movement. Images that are concrete and simple in structure provide an easy and safe beginning. Next, I would add images that stimulate kinesthetic response. Finally, introduce abstract images that draw on a student's experience and affect. The following examples illustrate images that stimulate responses at different levels, from the kinesthetic to the personal.

Indecision

- Select two spots in the room with some distance between them.
- Walk back and forth between the two spots.
- Continue walking back and forth, but walk a little faster.
- Now walk slowly, continue traveling between the two spots, sometimes fast, sometimes slowly. Change the intensity.
- Now as you continue moving between the two spots, keep the image of a person having great difficulty making a decision.
- Concentrate on the feeling of indecision. Let the movement happen.

  Comment. The use of two spots provides a specific framework. Walking back and forth is simple, and by changing the tempo you set up a kinesthetic involvement. This makes it easier to move right into the image of indecision that will probably evoke memories of personal experiences.

Shiny Metal and Shadows

- Following relaxation, sit in a comfortable position with your eyes closed.
- Have the image of a large piece of shiny metal. The sun is playing on the metal. There is a shimmering, bright sensation.

- Be clear about the image, then let it move. Let this develop for a while.
- Now, change the image to shifting shadows, floating clouds.
- Be aware of the feeling; let it move. Let this develop for a while.
- Now, shift from one image to the other, sometimes a shimmering sensation, sometimes floating clouds and shadows. Let it shift from one to the other as it wants to move.

Comment. This kind of image usually results in a study of contrasting qualities. It is based on a kinesthetic response and is safe to explore.

Tightrope

- Have the image of a tightrope, high off the floor. You are standing on the platform ready to try walking across.
- You want to do this but you are not sure that you can make it.
- Take time to get a clear image of the tightrope with you on the platform. Be aware of your feelings.
- When you are ready, begin your journey.
- You may encounter difficulties but you keep trying new approaches. Take your time and concentrate on the feeling.
- Let it move when you are ready.

Comment. If this experience is approached carefully, so that it does not become a mechanical act, most individuals become deeply involved. Usually the movement event takes on aspects of a personal journey or personal encounters. At this level of involvement, it becomes a dance study.

Attachment

- Have the image of a person attached to something: an idea; a person; a situation. I don't know what, but it is important.
- The attachment feels like a cord that binds or connects, but deep inside there is a desire to be released—to free one's self.

- Take a minute to be clear about the image and your feelings about the attachment.

- When you are ready, let the movement happen.

Comment. This is an abstract image that gives individuals freedom to arrive at their own image of attachment. The focus is on their response to interaction between the self and some outside force.

Entanglement in a Web

- Have an image of entanglement in a web; perhaps an insect, animal, or person caught in a web trying to get free, trying to find a way out.

- Concentrate on the image. Be very clear about the image and the feelings.

- Let the movement happen.

Comment. This image may evoke a response that is abstract based on qualities related to the struggle toward freedom. However, in some instances it triggers a very personal response as revealed in these statements taken from students' journals:

As I was caught in the web, I was recalling the experience of being tangled in my boyfriend's conservative family and environment. Feeling it spin fast, knowing that it was limiting me, but reluctant to take action against it. I attempted to deal with it. The harder I tried, the stickier and more painful it became. Spying an opening out of it, I squeezed through to go back and observe objectively. What had the web been doing to me? Paralyze me for the kill—now I was out and could toy with the absurdity of the small attempts to do me in. I could try the web on and wear it with style. But oh the web woos with subtle lines, so off with. It must be scrambled and wadded beneath my feet. What a hateful pleasure (Carol).

I am in a "mind web" so to speak—I saw the web in a sensing way. I believe the web was me, my life, my being, my world. I walked through the web and felt its attachment to my body. I tried to wipe the fibers off of me! I duck, dip, and meander through the complicated pattern: walking, turning, twisting. Then I reach out and pull one of the fibers to the side. I can change the pattern of the web. I

am happy with this realization. So now the journey through the web is much different. I am the one who has control of the web. Now I am aware that I am the one who is moving the fibers so that I can move through them. It's a whole new ballgame (Doris)!

After reading these accounts, you might wonder if movement studies accompanied by this kind of personal imagery and feelings should be considered choreography. No, probably not, but they do give external shape to one's imagery and internal sensations—the first step in forming. Imaginative thought processes such as these students have described represent an important stepping stone in the creative process. Obviously, the movement exploration opened the way for imagery, and these dancers were certainly involved in inner-sensing.

It would seem that we must first discover images and feelings at a very personal level and then gradually progress to the stage where the essence of felt experience is transformed in such a way that the resulting choreography has the power to evoke a response that is more universal in nature.

Group Movement Studies

The early improvisational experiences, such as those described in previous chapters, should be structured so that students have an opportunity to work alone. This is important in the beginning because the process demands that they give complete attention to inner-sensing and letting movement emerge spontaneously. Stimuli from another person at this point in the development is a distraction from the central task. Through individual work, students discover the real meaning of inner involvement and authentic response. When this discovery has been made and they are able to stay in touch with their own sensing and responding, then the opportunity to work with others is valuable: first in groups of two, then in groups of three, and finally in a larger group.

If improvisation is undertaken with other people before each student has developed the ability to let the movement happen intuitively and authentically, the result is apt to be contrived move-

ment, lacking in aesthetic substance, and of little value in further-ing creative development. In order to work successfully with others, each person must be able to sustain his or her concentration in relation to the motivation and at the same time tune in to the movement response of another person. So, improvising with other people requires that each dancer be able to respond concurrently to both inner and outer stimuli. The externalized movement flows spontaneously from the initial image or motivation and is also activated by the response to the movement of another person. When this happens successfully, the movement event resulting from this interactive process takes on a life of its own.

I find that some kind of preliminary movement preparation helps students to take hold of the image and respond spontaneous-ly. The preparation makes the transition to the new image seem natural and prevents any disruption in the flow of energy. The improvisational experience should build slowly, giving time for exploration of each phase of development. Some of the descriptive words are dropped in softly so that they blend with the ongoing process and serve as cues but not in a way that is disruptive. The facilitator must stay involved with the ongoing process so that word cues and suggestions for shifts in action mesh with the group's flow of movement. In a way you must become one of the group while assuming the role of facilitator.

The following improvisational studies are designed for in-dividuals working alone, or in groups of two, three, and five or more.

The Search

- Preparation: focus on isolated movements of the head.
- Let the head move in different ways, different angles. Have the feeling of trying to discover or locate something.
- Walk in different directions. Walk fast; then slow; sometimes fast and sometimes slow.
- Now imagine you're searching for something: a direction, a per-son, an answer, or yourself.

- Your feeling might be one of curiosity, anxiousness, fear, or impatience. Take time to be clear about your image and feeling. Then let the movement happen.

- Let it develop on its own.

Two Elderly People (group of two)

- Have the image of an old tree twisted and gnarled but still living and growing. Be clear about the feeling.

- Let the movement happen.

- Continue but join with another person, keeping the image of twisted and gnarled trees.

- Begin to feel a relationship with the other person. Keep in touch with the feeling of the gnarled tree still living and growing.

- Now shift the image to two elderly people. Have the image of the problems of age, people still functioning, relating, and connecting.

- Let the movement develop on its own.

Suspicion (group of three)

- While standing, become aware of your center, the long straight line down through the center of your head, through the torso, and down between the legs and into the ground. Repeat several times.

- Now feel the energy from the ground up through the torso and through the head. Repeat several times.

- Begin to explore your wrist moving different ways.

- Explore movement in the elbow and then in the shoulder.

- Now start with the other wrist, then the elbow and shoulder.

- Continue exploring movement in the hips, knees, and ankles. Then shift from one joint to another moving spatially.

- Let the movement take you into groups of threes facing each other.

- Have the image of a person who is suspicious.

- Each person has a feeling of distrust, uneasiness, suspicion.

- Take a minute to get in touch with the image and feeling then let the movement begin to happen.

- Keep the image of suspicion; let the feeling and movement intensify; let the movement develop on its own.

No Place to Hide (group of five or more)

- Take some position in different parts of the room.
- All imagine having no place to hide, feeling impending danger on all sides. You sense the need to escape.
- Begin to move by darting, running, sometimes freezing.
- Let the head and face be involved; shift your focus.
- Sometimes you may cluster in twos, threes, or in larger groups. Keep the image and feeling very clear.
- Feel the energy growing in intensity and let it develop in any way. Keep it alive until it finds it own ending.

Improvisational experiences play a basic role in the development of the choreographer and should be included in the overall design of creative education. More specifically, this intuitive and spontaneous response is useful in discovering movement ideas that provide the raw material for choreography. Also, group improvisational activities build a kind of sensitivity and inner-connectedness within the group. This contributes to the organic development in group choreography and the feeling of aliveness and authenticity.

Summary

Images and imagination play a critical role in the choreographic process. In fact, the creative thought process is dependent on a free flow of imagery.

In a special state of consciousness, the choreographer draws on memory traces from the current and past experiences that set in action a stream of images. Through a feed forward/feedback process, images and associated feelings unfold, shift, come together in new constellations, and continue shifting until the sought-after synthesis takes shape. The unfolding images and felt thought provide the foundation for the creative act.

Movement experiences motivated by images provide an effective means of gaining access to the imaginative thought process. Through guided experiences, students expand their ability not only to image, but also to let the unfolding images provide the stimulus for externalized movement. Heightened sensory awareness of images, and the feelings associated with those images, is critical in transforming sensory experience into motion that can be molded into a dance.

CHAPTER 5
Transforming

The success of the choreographer's creative work is dependent upon the imagination transforming inner experience into motion. The motion is not a simple gesture, everyday movement, technique, or pantomime; it is more. It is motion in the purest form that flows from an inner source imaginatively molded that produces an illusion—a kind of magical experience. The transforming of the feelings and images into motion, a qualitative substance, is an essential aspect of the creative process.

What is the nature of motion as qualitative substance? Basically, it is the material with which the artist works and is composed of sensuous elements, both visual and kinesthetic. Energy, space, and rhythm are inherent aesthetic elements in all motion. Every simple or complex pattern of motion has an energy flow, a spatial pattern, and a rhythmic structure. When the artist is successful in imaginatively articulating and molding these elements, the unfolding motion creates a transparency, or illusion that makes the creator's aesthetic goal available to the viewer. The transforming of the inner vision into a symbolic form is a critical phase of the creative process.

As Susanne Langer has stated: "The virtual form must be organic and autonomous, divorced from actuality. Whatever enters into it does so in radical artistic transformation: its space is plastic, its time

59

is musical, its themes are fantasy, its actions symbolic" (1953: 204). In the case of the experienced choreographer, this crucial process of transforming feelings and images happens intuitively. An inner impulse guides the outward flow of motion that incorporates inherent sensuous elements. Through an autonomous forming process, the qualitative substance is molded into an organic whole.

But what about the inexperienced choreographer? How does this individual discover the role of sensuous elements in transforming everyday experiences into symbolic forms? At first the concentration is on inner-sensing and allowing the movement to flow spontaneously, just letting it happen. These early creative outpourings gradually take shape as little entities. But during this early stage of development, the full kinesthetic awareness of sensuous elements is usually not a part of the young choreographer's experiences. Thus the energy, spatial, and rhythmic elements are used in a limited way. The question then is: How does one discover the role of the elements in transforming sensory experiences into art forms?

Obviously experience is a basic factor. Through repeated creative effort, students make new discoveries about the aesthetic process. However, the teacher plays a vital role in hastening the discovery. Through guided experiences and discussions about the finished form, the young artist can become aware kinesthetically of the wide range of possibilities in each element and the effect of various shadings on the aesthetic statement. These new discoveries are then stored as a part of his or her kinesthetic awareness and intuitively drawn upon as needed in the process of transforming the inner experience into outward form.

Guided experiences with a focus on sensuous elements may be set in action through the use of images, word cues, or visual and aural stimuli. They should be designed so that the students become deeply involved in the overall motivation and respond intuitively. In other words, students do not approach the task with a focus on a specific element, such as space, but rather the concentration is on the larger motivation that stimulates them to intuitively transform the inner experience into motion that embraces a new and expanded use of sensuous elements.

Because sensuous elements, such as energy, space, and rhythm, are inherent ingredients in all motion, they never exist in isolation. However, in the following section, the nature of each element is discussed for the purpose of clarification, and suggestions are made about ways to evoke responses that result in the imaginative use of each element.

Energy Flow

Movement happens when effort is expended. Without effort there can be no action—no sense of vitality. The amount of effort and the way the energy is released determines the expressive quality of each part of the movement. For example, a large amount of energy produces movement that is perceived as strong, while a small amount of energy results in movement that is sensed as weak. Within this polarity of weak to strong, there is the possibility of creating a great variety of shadings simply by altering the energy flow.

When the energy is released slowly and steadily, the movement is sensed as smooth and continuous. This feeling can be modified by releasing energy in different ways. For example, a small amount of energy released slowly may give the feeling of delicacy, fragility, or tentativeness, while a large amount of energy released slowly may be perceived as strong, aggressive, defensive, or determined.

When energy is released in spurts with pauses in between, the movement conveys quite a different feeling and may be sensed as disconnected or uncertain. When these bursts of energy happen in fast succession, the feeling is different than when there are pauses in between the bursts. The fast explosive bursts with pauses may give a feeling of uncertainty or impatience. The amount of energy, combined with speed and release, changes the qualitative character of the movement and thus makes possible a wide range of expressive possibilities. Therefore, an important aspect of the choreographer's experience is the discovery of the polarity of energy from weak to strong, and the many modifications that are possible. This awareness enables the choreographer to respond spontaneously with appropriate shadings of energy and specific dynamics according to what he or she is trying to express in the choreography.

Using a variety of movement dynamics may be difficult for many students. Each person tends to have a characteristic way of moving that reflects his or her personal style. Usually there is one type of energy flow and a way of moving that seems most natural. For example, one student may tend to move slowly with a smooth quality while another tends to move with lots of energy released in bursting patterns. The one who moves with lots of high energy in bursting patterns may find moving slowly and smoothly difficult. Likewise, the student who moves slowly and smoothly may be uncomfortable moving with lots of energy in a strong and explosive pattern. Though every individual has a typical way of moving, it is important that the choreographer become skilled in modifying energy output in a great variety of ways. This is essential for the full development of the range of expressive potential inherent in movement.

Becoming skilled in the use of energy as an aesthetic element requires more than participation in discussions or even exercises that call for the use of energy. One needs the opportunity to respond to movement tasks that encourage an inner-directed and sensitive use of dynamics. This implies transforming feelings into movement qualities that function as aesthetic elements. These movements will require various levels and intensities of energy. As a result, the dancers will discover how different levels of energy reflect a variety of emotional states. They can then use this knowledge to create more expressive dances.

The following examples illustrate how words and images can be used to evoke an impulse for movement that uses energy in a variety of ways.

Strong to Delicate

- Walk in various directions. Feel your foot making contact with the floor naturally, then pressing firmly.
- Now have the sense of crushing something with every step.
- Change the feeling to walking on something very fragile or delicate.
- Now shift from one sensation to the other, sometimes crushing, sometimes treading lightly as though walking on eggs.
- Continue walking. Transfer the crushing sensation to the hand and arms.
- Have a feeling of pressing into space; let the whole body become involved.
- Then change to the sensation of moving into space with a feeling of delicacy, fragility.
- Shift from one feeling to another; let it move into space and develop.

  Comment. The emphasis is on inner-sensing and the kinesthetic awareness that is developed while moving with different degrees of energy.

Hummingbird

- Sit in a comfortable position.
- Have the feeling of quivering or vibrating. Let one of your arms begin to move, keeping the feeling of quivering. Let one of your arms move around your body and out into space.
- Explore the sensation with either arm or both.
- Add the image of a hummingbird quivering, vibrating, and then pausing. Explore the image of the hummingbird: quivering, vibrating, pausing.
- Let it move in different ways.
- When it is ready, let the movement take you to your feet. Move freely in space.

Comment. The image of the hummingbird extends the possibility of improvisation and uses of energy in a spatial context. The sensation of quivering and vibrating involves different degrees of energy.

Pulled by a Rope

- Have the image of a heavy rope tied around your waist and fastened to the opposite corner of the room.
- Imagine that you are being pulled toward that corner. The pull is strong and you are resisting.
- Suddenly the pull changes and you are drawn to the opposite corner. Again, try to resist the pull.
- Now imagine that sometimes you are in control and pulling it. Then again, it is pulling you.

Comment. The focus is on experiencing in the body the feeling of a strong amount of energy and resistance. Shifting back and forth gives opportunity for imagery and improvisation.

Velvet Curtain

- Sit on the floor.
- Imagine that a large velvet curtain is in front of you. It extends up toward the ceiling and stretches to each side as far as you can reach. I don't know the color; perhaps, it is red, blue, or green. Have a clear image of the curtain and its color.
- Let one of your hands begin to move up and down feeling the velvet.
- Now let the other hand or both hands explore the texture of the velvet.
- Now, keeping the same sensation, let your hand move away from the curtain and move horizontally with the floor. Perhaps you have a feeling of gliding, like a swan floating on water.
- Let it move freely in space but keep the feeling of gliding, floating.
- Now change the feeling to darting quickly here and there, like a fish darting for food.

- Continue with a feeling of darting but let the movement take you to your knees and eventually to your feet.

- Now shift from one quality to the other as you wish. Give it freedom to move in space but keep your concentration on the feeling of darting and gliding.

- When you are ready let it come to a close.

Comment. The emphasis is on the sensory response to the texture, then it shifts to imagery that evokes different uses of energy: darting, or quick bursts of energy, then gliding, or smooth and sustained movements.

Spatial Design

All action set in motion by the dancer takes place in a spatial context. Each movement, a single gesture or complex pattern, has a spatial design that becomes an integral part of the overall aesthetic experience. The specific definition and use of space is determined by the choreographer. Movement may be confined to a small space or projected into a large space; it may be directed forward, sideways, or backward; it may move in a straight line or in curved paths, or expand up or down in relation to gravity.

The experienced choreographer works with space intuitively, as a part of the total forming process. But in order for this sensitive and intuitive way of working to happen, dancers must experiment with different spatial possibilities and, through these experiences, discover the role that spatial design plays in the transformation of an image into a dance.

My experience suggests that when a dancer becomes involved in the creative process, attending to inner-sensing and imaging, the tendency is to keep the movement close to the center of the body. These early self-directed movement responses are usually limited in dimension and direction so that the dancer does not use the full range of spatial options, such as small to big, near to far, and ranges in between.

No doubt self-imposed restrictions in the use of space are related to our feelings of vulnerability and the need to protect ourselves.

For most people, the process of getting in touch with their feelings and transforming them into externalized movement is a new experience. So it is not surprising that dance students are cautious and venture out slowly into the surrounding space. The question then is how to help them break through these self-imposed spatial barriers.

The dance teacher should recognize and respect these early responses, but at the same time guide experiences in such a way that students are able to take increasing risks and gradually feel comfortable in exploring a wide range of spatial possibilities. Movement tasks that focus on kinesthetic awareness of spatial dimension and direction are sensed as safe and provide a good place to begin. These can be followed by images that evoke the impulse to use a wide range of spatial options. The following examples illustrate how word cues and images can be used to stimulate exploration of spatial possibilities.

Straight Lines

- Walk in any direction, but keep a very straight line.
- Now change direction frequently, still keeping a straight line.
- Make some lines long and others short. Continue, but move faster.
- Make the change in direction sharp and direct.
- Continue exploring long and short straight lines at your own pace.

Curved Paths

- Move your arm in a curved path. Then, move it any way but in a curved path.
- Now let your whole body be involved in a curved sensation.
- Now keeping the sense of curve, begin to walk in curved paths.
- Let it take you into larger curves and sometimes smaller curves.
- Let the curves grow into circles both large and small.
- Continue exploring the circle moving anywhere in the room.

Make large, small, and overlapping circles, sometimes moving fast and sometimes slow.

Comment. Guided movement gives the opportunity for sensing and exploring direction.

Silk Ropes

- Sit on the floor.

- Have the image of large silk ropes hanging from the ceiling. The room is filled with these silky ropes of all colors: blue, red, green, and yellow.

- Have the image of ropes near you and then all through the room. See their size and color.

- When you are ready, begin to explore the ropes near you. Feel their texture. Move with them any way you want.

- Give yourself freedom to get on your knees or on your feet and eventually move about the room. Relate to the ropes in different ways.

- You may travel through them, or turn with them. Experience some as delicate, others as strong.

Comment. The image of silk ropes provides a sensory experience but also shifts attention to a larger spatial environment and stimulates moving out into space.

Three Spots

- In a standing position, have the image of three spots somewhere around you: in front, to the side, or in the back. One spot is high, one is at eye level, and the other is low. Have a clear image of where each spot is, how high it is and how far away.

- Take time to get a clear image of the spots and their relationship to you.

- When you are ready, begin to move in relation to these spots. Try to feel some connection between them.

- Each spot may have a different feeling, a different energy. Let the movement develop in its own way.

Comment. The image of different spots and different heights gives a structure for spatial exploration.

Three Poles

- Have the image of three poles like pillars. See them in some relationship to you. I don't know the height of the poles, or the color, or the texture. Perhaps they are not all the same distance from you.

- Take time to get a clear image of the poles and their relationship to you.

- They may appear as obstacles or as supports. What is the feeling associated with each pole?

- When you are ready, begin to move in relationship to the poles. Let the movement develop.

Comment. This image provides a spatial structure and encourages movement into space. The personal relationship that evolves will usually reflect different qualities.

Symmetrical / Asymmetrical

The shaping of the movement of a dancer or group of dancers is an important aspect of the overall spatial design in choreography. The specific ordering of the movement of a body or bodies is guided by the intent of the choreographer and the qualities desired. If the underlying feeling calls for stability, a sense of balance, security, calm, or repose, the spatial design of the body in motion will likely be symmetrical. But if the underlying feeling calls for tension, for interacting, shifting relationships, then the design of the body in motion will probably be asymmetrical. The asymmetrical design creates a feeling of being off-balance, just the opposite of the stability projected by symmetry. When used wisely, the asymmetrical type of spatial structuring creates interacting forces that stimulate a kinesthetic response in the audience.

Both symmetry and asymmetry have expressive potential. An important aspect of the learning experience is the discovery of the aesthetic value of each and how to use symmetry and asymmetry as an expressive factor, as well as a design factor. The first concern should be to recognize the difference in spatial structures and then to make this awareness become functional through the medium of movement.

Observing spatial structures in the environment can be a valuable experience. For example, observe the use of symmetrical and asymmetrical design in different buildings. What feeling does it give you? Then concentrate on the different aspects of nature that you encounter. Look for the asymmetrical structures. Notice details and try to discover the inner relationships in what you are observing. What feelings do you experience? Learning to see, perceive, and feel is basic to understanding the aesthetic value of different types of design. Observations such as these should be followed by discussion. The opportunity to share what one has observed often helps to clarify the discovery. The individual who has not yet learned to see clearly and sense the relationships existing within a structure will find this discussion illuminating.

Rhythmic Structure

Choreography, when it is successful, appears to have a life of its own. The projected sense of vitality reveals a movement happening that is always in transition, going from one event to another. Dance, like the living organism, is perpetuated by a continuous pattern of changes. The successive beginnings and endings of these changes create an internal rhythm. The rhythmic structure, unique in each work, grows out of the specific function of the movement event.

We are familiar with the ever-present rhythms of our bodies. For example, the breath rhythm (the taking in and giving out of air), the heartbeat (with its systolic and diastolic phases), and the foot rhythm (the up and down of each step as the body relates to gravity) are all rhythms that are intrinsic to our beings. We are aware of the recurring rhythms that exist in nature, such as the ebb and flow of the tide and the rise and fall of the geyser. So it is with dance. The inner impulse activates the release of energy in segment after segment of movement. The recurring beginnings and endings in the unfolding movement event sets up an underlying pulse and rhythmic structure. This internal rhythm creates a dynamic that contributes significantly to the continuity, integration, and perception of the dance form and thus to its aesthetic significance.

The fully developed use of rhythmic structure evolves with experience. I have found that, during the beginning period when students are concentrating on attending to inner-sensing (feelings and images), the externalized movement is usually characterized by a slow continuous flow of energy. This, however, is an important stage in their development because it indicates that the students are involved and responding at a felt level. The movement is not intellectually contrived.

As students are able to sustain concentration on inner-sensing and let the movement happen spontaneously, new developments in the rhythmic structure will begin to occur. For example, you may notice that some body part, perhaps a hand or foot, begins to move at a faster pace or in an irregular pattern with definite accents. As students gain confidence and are able to risk responding freely to the inner impulse, their externalized movements will begin to incorporate varied and more complex rhythmic patterns. When the choreographer is working at a deeply involved level and allowing the intuitive process to guide the forming of the movement event, the rhythmic structure will evolve organically and be an integral part of the dance. This development is illustrated by a student's description of his discovery of a new use of body parts through the rhythmic response:

I recall that my previous movement has been mostly in the upper body. Today the key was the hummingbird image—weightless and swift—effortless movement in space. Yes, much more spatial—much more strength in the movement and use of the whole body. A nice strange feeling to notice the feet in motion. Previously I put them in motion. Could be that I am beginning to find my legs and feet through spontaneous rhythm (Jack).

The student's progress from movement that is characterized by a slow and continuous energy flow to varied and complex rhythmic structures is facilitated by movement tasks that inspire a wide range of rhythmic experiences. These would include speeds that range from slow to fast, durations that are short or long, and effort patterns that are even or uneven, as well as shadings between these polarities. I try, first, for discovery that comes from experience and then later give a verbal explanation. This method seems more functional and supports the organic development.

Another type of experience that involves observation and listening can be valuable. For example, attending to specific encounters in the environment, such as the rhythmic characteristics of trees being blown by the wind, birds in flight, songs of birds, or machines in the process of work, can be used as motivation for movement studies. The focus of the creative response is on the rhythmic structure.

The ultimate goal is to develop an awareness of rhythmic possibilities so that, during spontaneous and intuitive moments of creativity, the rhythmic pattern takes shape as an integral part of the dance form. The following examples suggest ways to facilitate the use of rhythm as an aesthetic element of movement.

Word Patterns

Tell me: "How long must I wait?" or "Who said that it couldn't be done?"

- Say the words in an even rhythm, one word after another.
- Then say them again placing emphasis on different words, changing speed.
- Continue as a group but work independently. Each person explores saying the words with different feelings and speeds.
- The clatter of all the different voices frees the individual to experiment with different emotional responses.
- Continue exploring the words and let the feet pick up the rhythm.
- Gradually let the arms and body begin to move in response to the

rhythm. Continue exploring various ways of saying the words. Let the whole body become involved.

Comment. This can be a fun exploration that frees the students to try various rhythmic structures.

Sounds

- In a standing position, have the group say "Ah," letting the sound continue with the output of breath. Repeat several times.
- Continue softly letting the breath out as you say the sound "Ah."
- Let it move anywhere in the room; concentrate on the breath flow with the sound.
- Now explore different ways of making the sound, sometimes higher in pitch, or lower, sometimes faster, or slower. Take time to explore variations.
- Be aware of the group sound. Let the sounds begin to relate as a choral group in a moving choir.
- Let the group move spatially taking their time letting the flow take them. The sound and movement should develop on its own.
- Let it gradually find its own ending.

Comment. The use of sound and breath offers opportunity to explore a variety of rhythmic patterns, the relationship of breath to movement, and group experience. But in order to be effective, students must be ready to concentrate at a deeply involved level.

Scurrying and Freezing

- Sit or stand. Have the image of an insect, a little creature, or person scurrying away seeking safety. Have the feeling of fright and the need to escape.
- Let the hands or feet move; sometimes scurry away then freeze, or move cautiously.
- Let the whole body become involved.
- Gradually let it come to a close.

Comment. The feeling of scurrying, freezing, and moving cautiously evokes movement of an uneven duration and different rhythmic structures.

Birds in Flight

* Feel your feet connected to the earth. Sense the energy coming up one leg, across the pelvis, and down the other leg. Repeat several times.

* Now sense the energy coming up both legs, through the torso, the center of the head, and above into space. Repeat several times.

* Be aware of the incoming breath as the energy travels up the body and the outgoing breath with the release of energy.

* As the energy comes up, let it go into the arms and carry them upward, then release. As the energy travels up through the arms into space, have the feeling of lightness, being lifted.

* Let it move into space.

* Now have the image of birds in flight. Let it move in any direction.

* Keep the concentration on breath and energy flow.

* Have the feeling of floating—sometimes moving quickly. Let it develop and find its own ending.

Comment. This leads to a group improvisation with an underlying breath rhythm. Individuals must be ready to work at an involved level in order for the image to be effective.

Summary

It is essential that the choreographer understand the role that energy, rhythm, and space play in creating the desired dynamics within a dance form. One way of acquiring this understanding is to experience each of the elements through improvisation stimulated by images. This discovery process contributes to an awareness and foundation that can be drawn on freely. The easy use of the polarities of movement elements—weak and strong, slow and fast, small and big, and the shadings in between—is critical to the autonomous forming of movement.

Though each of the movement components—energy flow,

rhythmic structure, and spatial design—have been discussed as separate elements, they never, in fact, exist in isolation. Movement that we observe in the dance performance always happens as the result of a specific energy output, has a definite rhythmic structure, and spatial design. This holds true for simple or complex movement patterns.

A critical phase of artistic activity is the transforming of the sensory input and imaginative thought into movement that embodies the qualities inherent in the envisioned dance form. First, there is the taking in (seeing, sensing, feeling, imaging) and then the transforming of felt thought and inner vision into an externalized form. It is the sensitive articulation of aesthetic elements that gives the unfolding movement event its dynamic quality and sense of vitality.

CHAPTER 6

Forming

How a piece of choreography or any piece of art comes into being is somewhat of a mystery. Integration, craft, and hard work of course are requisites, but there is more. What happens during the involved period of creating, when the inner process takes over and guides the forming of the externalized work of art? This phase of the process is difficult to explain. Artists speaking about their work often say that they don't know where it comes from. Something just wells up; it's inexplicable.

Sybil Shearer, a choreographer, when asked how her dances come into being, thought a moment and then replied, "I open myself—wait. It just comes." Speaking about the inexplicable part of the process, Aaron Copland, the musician, has stated, "The source of the germinal idea is one phase of the creative process that resists rational explanation. All we know is that the moment of possession is the moment of inspiration . . . whence it comes or in what manner it comes, or how long its duration, one can never tell" (1959: 52). Joseph Campbell has stated, "Anyone writing a creative work knows that you open, you yield yourself, and the book talks to you and builds itself" (1988: 58).

What is fascinating about the creative process is our ability to get in touch with an inner source, an inner voice that takes over and guides the unfolding of the externalized form. During this phase of the creative act, when inspiration takes over, an autonomous form-ing process transforms experiences and inner vision into a meta-morphic image. This autonomous forming process happens when the creator is in a state of relaxed concentration and a special mode of thought. The focus is on inner experiencing and the scanning and searching for completion.

During an interview with choreographer Alwin Nikolais, I asked if he was functioning at another level of consciousness when he was involved with creativity. His immediate reply was, "Oh yes!" Dis-cussing the way his creative ideas come into being he said, "It speaks. I have the feeling of the germinal seed and, once you have discovered the seed, it has a character that dictates its own con-tinuity. Once you understand that, you allow it to grow on its own. You don't choreograph—just stay out of its way."

Professional artists describe their experience during the intense moments of creating in different ways, but running through all their comments is the recognition that an inner-directed intuitive process, often referred to as inexplicable, guides the discovering and shaping of the aesthetic form. The germinal material that emerges from the inner-oriented process provides the unique substance embodied in the work of art. Artists may use their craft to further develop and refine certain aspects of the intuitively created form, but the original structure does seem to hold.

Craft plays a significant role in choreographing, but without the germinal material that flows from the imaginative and intuitive process, the final product will lack a sense of authenticity. As Murray Louis told me, "Craft is important but it is like making a lovely object. If you don't have the right marble, it doesn't matter how skilled a stonecutter you are, you are going to lose something of the special quality of the marble."

Artists pursue their art for different reasons. Sometimes the goal is simply to create an art form that is aesthetically satisfying, other times the work grows out of an inner need to clarify certain elements of their experience. But regardless of the specific motiva-tion, the artist's concern is always to make a statement with form.

Giving form to what we see, perceive, feel, and imaginatively conceive is a persistent human need. An inner urge prompts us to organize elements of our experience into meaningful wholes, make order out of disorder, and create form out of chaos. We see this tendency in our everyday behavior. For example, we will rearrange objects and furniture in our homes and then say, "That's better." Or we may reorganize plants and flowers in the garden so that they *feel right*. And so it is with our day-to-day encounters. We strive to bring varied experiences together so that they make sense, and clarify our relationship to the world. This inward search for order results in a process we know as *symbolization*. The process of symbolization is satisfying in and of itself, but in a larger sense it serves a very basic human need: a need to give form to our experience, which in turn provides a means of knowing, expressing, and communicating.

Ben Shahn's (1957) description of how his painting *Allegory* came into being illustrates how a specific event can trigger a need to bring past and present experiences together. Underlying this process is the search for truth.

Shahn states that "the immediate source of the painting of the red beast was the Chicago fire in which a colored man [named Hickman] had lost his four children." Shahn was asked to make a drawing to accompany the newspaper story of the fire. After making many sketches, he settled on one that he describes as "a highly formalized wreath of flames with which I crowned the plain shape of the house which had burned."

After the newspaper assignment was completed, Shahn could not dismiss the Hickman story. He felt that he had not expressed the enormity of the fire and its tragic aftermath. This particular fire had aroused in him a chain of personal memories, especially of two great fires he experienced as a child. One was a fire that destroyed a Russian village in which his grandfather lived. He was there and watched the bucket brigades attempt to save the village. The other fire was the one that burned his family's home. All of their belongings were destroyed, and his parents were stricken beyond the power to recover. Over a period of months, Shahn made many sketches before he envisioned the final painting. He states, "When I at last turned the lion-like beast into a painting I felt able to imbue it with everything I had felt about a fire. I incorporated the highly formalized flames from the Hickman story as a terrible wreath around its head, and under its body I placed four children, figures which to me hold the sense of all the helpless and innocent. The image that I sought to create was not one of a disaster; that somehow does not interest me. I wanted instead to create the emotional tone that surrounds a disaster; you might call it the inner disaster" (1957: 32, 33, 37).

Does this same process that the artists speak about hold true for all people? Is the autonomous forming process available to the young choreographer as a way of ordering experience and making an aesthetic statement? Undoubtedly the answer is yes.

Individual Creative Development

One of our unique characteristics is the ability to respond creatively and to form experience through some means of symbolization. The difference between the professional artist and the inexperienced choreographer is a matter of experience and the level of creativity that may be attained. But every individual has the potential to respond creatively and give external form to feelings and images.

Henry Schaeffer-Simmern has illustrated how an individual's hidden creative potential can be released and developed. In his book, *The Unfolding of Artistic Activity* (1961), he describes his work with inexperienced individuals of different backgrounds: delinquents, mentally ill people, refugees, and business people. Using the medium of the visual arts, he started work by asking individuals to draw something that was of interest to them. The first drawings were very simple, sometimes no more than an outline. After discussion of each drawing with the individual, he suggested that they continue with another drawing. He never gave negative criticism. After working for several months in an environment that was supportive and encouraged self-directed activity, individuals made dramatic progress. Each new drawing growing out of the same subject matter showed increased visual perception and skill, as well as impressive development in the use of imaginative ideas and a sense of form.

Can a similar creative growth process happen for the inexperienced person through the medium of dance? I am convinced that it can.

During my work with children and adults, I have seen dramatic development in their creative growth. These experiences reinforced my belief that all individuals have an innate sense of form. When the opportunity for appropriate experiences in self-directed activity is available, individuals will discover an inner source, a kind of magical force, that guides the shaping of movement into aesthetic forms. As an illustration, let me summarize the stories of Julia and Jerry.

Julia

Julia, a patient in a neuropsychiatric hospital, attended weekly movement sessions for eight months. My goal was to assist her in developing her creative potential. The sessions were designed to increase sensory awareness, facilitate self-directed action, and provide opportunity for giving form to her imaginative ideas.

The sessions included the use of basic movement experiences (skip, run, swing, leap, turn, etc.) and images that evoked imaginative response. Attention was given to aesthetic qualities inherent in the movement—the energy, rhythm, and spatial elements. We worked in a nonjudgmental environment.

One day, after we had been working for a few weeks, she asked if she could make a dance about a fish. (I had not talked about making dances.) The fish dance was followed by improvisations motivated by the images of a variety of creatures: a mouse, a snake, a horse, a swan.

Following each improvisation, she asked for my comments. I talked about the movement ideas and qualities that I had observed. Sometimes I offered suggestions about ways she might explore different qualities. For example, following the swan improvisation, I asked: "What would happen if the swan was unhappy and ignored by its friends?" She listened, thought for a while, then proceeded to improvise a new dance that had a very different feeling.

During the following weeks, a variety of images were used. One day I brought in a poem about the wind. After hearing the poem she said, "I'll make a dance about wind, rain, and a tornado."

Week after week she made steady progress. Her imaginative ideas started to flow freely, and the improvisations were sustained for longer periods of time. There was an obvious shift from the early improvisations of short durations, such as the first dance, to longer improvisations.

The highlight of her creative work happened during our next to last session. I brought in a Japanese fan for her to use as motivation and suggested the possibility of using the qualities of the fan in a butterfly dance. She said, "I'll do a Japanese dance." She started moving along a diagonal path using stereotypical fanning movements, then stopped suddenly and said, "I feel silly." She tried once more and then said, "I want to do what I want to do."

She positioned herself across the room on her hands and knees with her body close to the floor. Her head and arms were tucked under. She asked the musician to play and then started moving. The little elbows tried to work their way out and then returned. Gradually the movement took her to her knees and then to the feet. She started moving in a large circular pattern. The arms were moving as though attempting to balance and fly, and then the movement would falter and fall back to the knees. The effort to fly continued to gain strength, and the movement became more developed. Occasionally faltering and then regaining balance, she continued the development. After completion of the circular pattern and reaching a climax that suggested freedom to fly, she ended the movement in the original position on the floor. She stayed there quietly for a few minutes then sat up and looked at me. We had both experienced an unusual happening.

Obviously she had used my suggestion of the butterfly, starting from the cocoon, emerging, and finally returning. The significance of the event was what happened for her in the process. It was apparent that she had arrived at a new stage of development. She had allowed an inner process to guide the unfolding of her imaginative ideas and the shaping of the dance. The inner structure of her dance was more complex than her previous creations. She had created an aesthetic form that had the power to convey her unique statement.

Jerry

Jerry, a patient in a neuropsychiatric institution, attended a weekly movement session for seven months. He was a tall, slender, ten-year-old boy. He seldom initiated conversation but would respond to my suggestions. His tendency was to just follow directions; that seemed to be the easiest way to cope with life. His body coordination and basic movement skills were poor, including a very limited cross-extensor reflex. My goal was to assist him in gaining a more effective use of his body, in becoming more self-directed, and in developing his creative potential.

The sessions included basic movement skills and modifications that involved change in direction, quality, and speed. Sometimes we would use drum beaters as extensions of the arm. Sitting on the floor with a beater in each hand, we would beat rhythmic patterns on the floor. I would suggest different qualities and use of space, which he would explore. He loved the beaters and often asked to use them. After several sessions, he was able to start improvising on the floor, then go to a standing position while keeping the beaters in action. I would suggest that he try to use different body movements while he was doing the rhythmic beating. He would respond with a new improvisation using the body more fully in a larger spatial context.

Concerned about the cross-extensor reflex, I asked if he knew how to do an underhand softball pitch. He said "Yes." So we went through the motion of an underhand pitch with one hand and stepping forward with the opposite foot. This was repeated on the other side. As a follow-up, I brought a strong elastic band made into a loop two feet long. He would place the elastic under one foot, holding it with the opposite hand, then lift the elastic pulling the foot upward and take a step forward. This continued while moving around the room. After several repetitions, the action was reversed using the other foot and hand. He liked this game-like movement, and it reinforced the use of arm-leg opposition.

Images were used frequently as a means of motivating imaginative movement responses. One day I suggested that we use the image of an insect. He said, "You mean a bee?" When I asked him how a bee moved, he replied, "It flies, hovers, and turns around." He then proceeded to improvise movement growing out of that image. In the following weeks, we explored a variety of images including a bird in a box and a tug of war. These early improvisations were usually of short duration and rather limited in the use of movement.

One day, I suggested the image of making a decision. He said "You mean a choice?" Sitting on the floor with legs crossed he explored pulling, gathering motions on one side and then the other side. He continued alternating sides, but with little variation in the movement. The next session I suggested that we try the image of choice. We talked about how difficult it is sometimes to make a choice and the feelings that one has. This time he started in a standing position. The improvisation that followed was longer, used a greater variety of movement, and had a feeling of development and wholeness. At the end of the session, I asked what he liked best today. He replied, "Making a choice."

During the early part of the session, I included basic movement patterns, concentrating on energy, rhythm, and spatial possibilities. We did this informally moving about in the room. One day after all those weeks of dutifully following my suggestions, he took over the leadership and started giving me directions: "Try going sidewards"; "Now skip backward"; "Could you do a turn?"; "Do a do-si-do"; "Now do whatever your heart desires"; and on and on. I immediately reversed roles and followed his lead until he tired and stopped. I felt that this was a real breakthrough. Instead of just following along as had been his pattern, he took the leadership role and gave movement suggestions while continuing his own movement.

Over the months, he had made steady progress. He moved with greater freedom and spontaneity. He sustained improvisations for a longer period of time. The movements were more imaginative and conveyed different qualities. Even though I had observed these changes, I was not prepared for the stunning development that occurred during our last session.

I usually brought a bag with different objects that were used for motivation. He looked in the bag and took out a Japanese fan, opened it, and started a fanning motion. Then he said, "I'll make a fan dance."

He went to the other side of the room, sat on the floor with legs crossed. He opened the fan, looked at it for several minutes, then started a fanning motion first in one hand and then the other hand. As the fanning continued, he got to his feet and started moving forward in a large circular path using a hopping action. The fanning movement never stopped, always shifting from one hand to the other.

As he progressed around the circle, his feet started moving in different rhythmic patterns, the energy level grew stronger, and the hopping action increased in elevation. While these new developments were happening with the feet and legs, the fanning motion never ceased. Gradually the movement took him back to the starting point where he slowly returned to the original sitting position. The fanning action continued first in one hand and then the other, gradually slowing and coming to an end.

He sat quietly for a few minutes looking at the fan, then got up and came over to where I was sitting. Quiet but obviously moved by the experience, he said, "I liked my fan dance."

I too was quiet and very moved by what had just happened. He had made his own statement with form. This young boy who started with poor coordination and little imaginative response had just created his dance—a simple form that had a beginning, a development with interesting rhythmic structure, and an ending.

Teaching Strategies

How do the experiences of these children and Schaeffer-Simmern's (1961) work with adults relate to the teaching of choreography? What are the implications? I believe that, in order for the ultimate creative growth in artistic activity to happen for the beginning dancer, a fresh approach to teaching is required. This approach is based on the belief that every individual has inner resources and a sense of form that is lying dormant—just waiting to be released and nourished. This is not to say that every individual can become a great artist, but rather that everyone has creative potential and can achieve in the area of artistic activity. The teacher must view this work as a process, with dancers progressing to deeper levels of understanding as they work through the steps of creating a new work of art. As the following chart shows, there is a definite progression to this growth in creativity, although it will vary for each individual.

Creative Process

Taking in	experiencing a range of sensory data ——————▶	ever widening and deepening
Feeling	getting in touch with bodily felt sense ——————▶	inner listening with greater sensitivity
Imaging	becoming aware of images ——————▶	images emerge and interact freely
Transforming	transforming feelings, images into movement ——————▶	movement used metaphorically
Forming	synthesizing of inner experience ——————▶	intuitive forming of felt thought

Developmental pattern: unique for each individual

Working from this point of view, the role of the teacher of choreography is not one of pouring in, but rather one of bringing out. As the creative work progresses, indirect teaching can assist students in becoming aware of significant concepts, such as the role that simplicity (economy), unity, and function play in the successful achievement of the envisioned art work. This awareness will lead to editing, or selecting, and the further development of movement ideas. Acting as a facilitator, the teacher is concerned with releasing, enriching, and encouraging students so that they are motivated to set their own goals and control their creative activity.

Various experiences that provide a preparation for creating dance forms have been discussed in the preceding chapters. These have included movement tasks that assist the students in getting in touch with inner resources: feeling, imaging, and the transforming of felt experience into externalized movement events. Now the question is: How does the teacher facilitate the transition from the foundation experiences to the process of creating mature dance forms?

I have found that the continued use of images, especially more abstract, open-ended images, stimulates imaginative thought that leads to more mature creative work. Along with the experiential work, I include relevant visual material (films, videos, photographs) that heightens awareness of form and stimulates self-motivation. Images such as the following can be useful in preparing the inexperienced choreographers to undertake independent creative work motivated by their own intent and aesthetic goal.

Illusive Something

- Have an image of something illusive. I don't know what it is—perhaps an object, some achievement, a person?
- You are trying to capture it, but you never quite connect.
- There may be sudden changes, sudden moves, quiet periods.
- It could be serious or humorous.

- Take time to get a clear image of what it is; then let the movement happen.

Abstract Photograph

Select some photograph that will convey feeling and motivate movement. I have found the abstract photographs of Barbara Morgan very useful, for example, her *Pure Energy and Neurotic Man* (1972: 117).

- Look at the photograph. What do you feel? What kind of movement flow do you experience?

- What are the dominant movement characteristics? Do you see any inherent relationships? Does it convey any statement to you?

- Study the photograph. When you are ready, find your own space and begin exploring the feelings and qualities. Take your time. Let the movement happen.

Shroud

Provide students with a variety of materials, in pieces about 36-inches square of different colors and different textures. Ask them to select one. As preparation, discuss the various meanings of a shroud: as a garment of death; as a scrim or mask; as a means of concealing; a form of shelter; shrouded in mystery.

- Place the material over your head. Consider what meaning it has for you. Take time to get into the feeling.

- Allow images to form. Give yourself freedom to explore the feeling and images. Let the movement just happen.

- At some point, let it develop into its own form.

Beginning Choreography

Images will evoke memories of personal experiences, which in turn provide the impulse for movement. When dancers are able to sustain a relaxed concentration, allow images to emerge, shift, recombine, and let the unfolding movement ideas form organically, it is time to begin exploring their own ideas for choreography.

Some dancers will be anxious to explore their own ideas while others may be vague and need time to arrive at a real motivation for choreography. But regardless of their state of clarity, it is important that they have an opportunity to focus on their own ideas, feelings, and images: in other words, what *they* want to make dances about. I have implied that the early creative experiences should be undertaken by dancers working alone rather than in groups. I believe that dancers must first discover their own inner resources and learn to respond at the intuitive level before undertaking group projects. Each individual must become well grounded in the creative process and be able to create dance forms that are organic and authentic; this requires independent work. Later, there comes a time when the individual is ready to explore creating for twos, threes, or larger groups. This happens when the choreographer needs more than one body to give shape to his or her idea or image. This is the time for learning about forming group dances through discussion and visual materials. Group improvisation as a parallel experience can be valuable as a means of furthering spontaneity and intuitive response.

The first dance studies will probably be short and simple in idea and structure. In fact, one should expect such results in the early work. However, these early studies play an important role, because it is only through the repeated experience of creating your own dances that you grow. With experience, students will become more skillful in transforming images and feelings into movement that takes shape as an aesthetic form. However, the inexperienced choreographer must have time to discover and progress at a rate that is appropriate; creative growth cannot be rushed.

Developmental Growth

Henry Schaeffer-Simmern's research shows clearly that the unfolding of the artistic activity is developmental in nature. The simple structure precedes the complex form. He believed, "The incentive for such growth lies in the creator's innermost compulsion to proceed to a clear and richer visual cognition by independent visual judgment of his work. Through this process each successive stage of artistic configuration prepares thoroughly the condition for the formation of the next stage" (1961: 198).

The creative work of the choreographer, like that of the visual artist, is developmental in nature. This suggests that choreography students should have the opportunity to progress through the various stages of development at their own pace. They must have the opportunity to make mistakes and gradually discover how to progress from a simple structure to a complex form.

My observation of the unfolding of artistic growth as revealed in dance studies suggests that the young choreographer progresses through several stages. These are not arbitrary stages, and the suggested characteristics in each stage do not always apply because the unfolding of artistic activity is never identical in any two people. However, these stages do suggest a trend in creative development and imaginative forming of movement ideas.

Spontaneous movement is a key element in the first stage. This movement is confined to the space immediately surrounding the body. Energy is released in an even, continuous flow. There is little variety in the quality or intensity of the movement, and the dance tends to be short. There is no overriding form to the dance work; rather the movement comes in a continuous stream, with no beginning, middle, or end.

In the second stage, movement flows from deep involvement with the movement event itself. Now, the movement ideas have some development; there is a relation among the movement impulses. There is an increased use of space and more venturing out in different directions. Finally, a rudimentary form begins to manifest itself over the dance.

Feelings or vivid images come to the fore in the third stage of development. An increased vitality is immediately apparent in the movement, with the dancer making use of a wider variety of body parts. Phrases, or linked movement segments, begin to take shape. There is an increased use of energy, space, and rhythm. The form of the dance arises organically from the feelings portrayed.

Finally, there is a mature capability to transform images or feelings into dance movement. Ideas now are more complex, going beyond the initial stimulus; the focus of the dance is on the essence of the experience. Dynamics are employed to portray a wider range of emotions. While there is an increased use of movement throughout the body, there is also an overall integration of this movement so that it is not merely random. The form of the dance is more complex and develops organically, with a clear rhythmic structure.

During the early stage of creative development, the motivation and impulse for movement tends to grow out of the dancer's personal concerns. The externalized dance event is self-oriented and reflects an effort toward self-identification.

With increased experience, the choreographer's ability to perceive personal experiences in relation to the experiences of others grows. Sensing and awareness occur in a larger context. Emphasis shifts from the personal to a desire to share and communicate. The creative work reveals an organic development of form with a life of its own.

The third phase of creative development is characterized by a search for the essence or truth of what is deeply sensed. Through an organic process, the dance form takes shape as an integrated whole and acts as a symbol. The choreographer's motivation reaches beyond his or her immediate personal concern and becomes an independent force. As Lewis Mumford has stated: "The aesthetic symbol becomes detached from the immediate life of the artist. . . . The artist's self dissolves into the work of art and transcends the limitation of his personality and culture" (1952: 29).

I observed this developmental pattern again and again in the experimental choreography class. Though the time required to progress through the various stages would vary for different individuals, the pattern was always the same. This growth pattern is illustrated in the following summary of a student's first three dances.

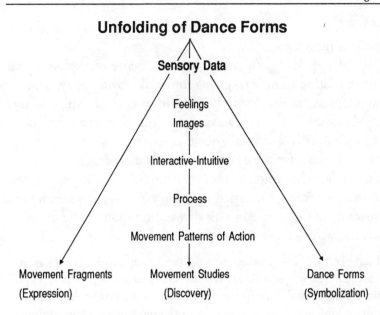

Unfolding of Dance Forms

Sensory Data

Feelings
Images

Interactive-Intuitive

Process

Movement Patterns of Action

Movement Fragments | Movement Studies | Dance Forms
(Expression) | (Discovery) | (Symbolization)

Ken's First Dance Studies

Throughout the first weeks of class, Ken was quiet, listening intently, and observing carefully. Though he approached the early experiences cautiously, it was apparent that he was deeply committed to the class experience. Gradually he was able to respond more freely and allow the spontaneous movement to flow from an inner impulse. As he stated in his journal: "I've been slowly beginning to understand and enter into the process. At first, my movements were manipulated, forced and I couldn't seem to free myself from the parent in my head. Now I am just starting to trust my own creative potential and to trust the process."

His first dance study grew out of personal feelings that evoked physical and emotional images. Attending to these feelings and images, he let the movement flow spontaneously and take its own shape. Though the final study was improvisational in nature and short in duration, it was successful in conveying a real sense of authenticity, a congruency between the inner-sensing and the externalized movement.

His second dance was motivated by a desire to explore movement in relation to gravity, giving into and moving away. This led to an increased awareness of weight and its control, which in turn evoked improvisations involving fall-and-recovery-type movements. Gradually a central theme of controlling and letting go became the basis for the development of the dance.

Following a discussion in class on continuity and its relationship to form, he became interested in form, especially sequencing and connecting as they related to his dance. In his journal he made the following statement:

> I have come to the conclusion that the forming process is similar in nature to the way one finds material. One usually improvises, plays with images and movement ideas. It is a nonjudgmental time, during which one seeks to remain in the right-brain, off-conscious state. In the same way, once a fair amount of material is found, one should improvise, play, and explore possible aspects of formal design. Just as one finds material one can find an overall form without being analytical or intellectual. One must first trust the fact that the same process that produces material will also elicit and shape it.

When this second dance was completed and performed in the lab-theater, he gave it the title *Loosely Held*. His costume was a dress shirt and slacks with soft black shoes. As one viewed the dance it was apparent that the underlying theme of controlling and letting go had been abstracted in such a way that the resulting movement captured the essence of those opposing pulls that one experiences in life. The early improvisations had taken shape so that the dance had a feeling of continuity and wholeness as well as inner substance.

At this point, he was encouraged by his progress and wanted to explore a different approach to choreography. He decided to start at a purely kinesthetic level and see what would emerge. He brought a piece of white cloth (one square yard) to class and

explored many ways of using it in movement. Lying on the floor he pulled, twisted, spread open the cloth in ever changing patterns that involved the body in a variety of ways: sitting, standing, and moving in space. This kind of exploration went on for weeks and as he later stated: "slowly the movement material emerged and along with it flashes of insight into the underlying motivation."

Finally the dance was completed. On the day of the showing, he came dressed in black leotard and tights, wearing a plastic face mask and carrying the white cloth. As he performed the dance it was evident that the early kinesthetic explorations, the twisting and pulling of the white cloth, had developed into a tightly formed dance. It possessed a powerful underlying emotional content that seemed related to his Asian-American background. He had not talked about his motivation and simply used the title *White Cloth*. For me the dance evoked images associated with the internment of Japanese-Americans during World War II. After class, when I talked with him about his intent, he said that he wasn't sure.

He continued working with the piece that was later presented in the lab-theater. By this time the underlying intent was clear to him, and he asked that the following statement be included in the program:

> This dance symbolizes the struggle of innocent people during World War II on both sides of the Pacific Ocean, from the survivors of Hiroshima and Nagasaki, to the internment of Japanese-Americans who lived along the Pacific Coast in the United States.

These three dances reveal the human tendency to progress from the personal to the more abstract and symbolic use of movement. The first dance, growing out of immediate personal feelings, provided the impulse for a spontaneous flow of movement. The movement event was short in duration but revealed a deep level of involvement and sense of wholeness. The second dance, *Loosely Held*, which was based on a specific motivation, had a greater development of movement ideas and clear phrasing. The form evolved organically and gave the feeling of continuity and wholeness.

In the third dance, *White Cloth*, the movement ideas were developed more fully. Ken made sensitive use of dynamics in his movements. The careful articulation of movement material resulted in a form that was more complex and symbolic in nature. The dance had the power, in contrast to the first study, to evoke an imaginative and aesthetic response in the observer.

The growth process of the choreographer might be characterized in two ways: first, a gradual understanding of symbol making through the imaginative use of movement, and, secondly, a gradual transition in perception that makes possible the transforming of personal experience into an aesthetic product that has the power to evoke a response that is more universal.

Lab-Theater Presentation

Throughout the developmental period, students should have frequent opportunity to show their dances as works-in-progress. This gives the choreographer a chance to perform the dance in a space comparable to a stage area. I do not see this as a time for criticism but rather as a time to try out and to share. Follow-up discussion should be positive and reinforcing, perhaps focusing on the student's progress and sections of the movement that seem especially effective.

When students have progressed to the point where their dances are developed as aesthetic forms and convey a clear, unique statement with a degree of clarity, then there is real value in providing an opportunity for an informal presentation in a lab-theater setting. Dance is a performing art, and dancers should have an opportunity to bring their choreography to full realization. Such a presentation requires thinking about the right title for the dance, deciding on an appropriate costume (even a simple one), working with stage lighting (even though minimal), and working with a musician who will provide improvised accompaniment. Such a presentation removes the work from the studio and opens the way for a beginning experience in theater presentation.

I have found that this kind of informal performing experience deepens the students' commitment to their creative work. The students offered these comments about this aspect of the class:

> Having a showing or performance in the lab-theater at the end of class was a great motivator and really helped me to zone in on what I was trying to do. We all know how costume, lighting, and staging affect the overall mood of the dance, but seldom do we really think about it while still in the early choreographic process. Having the opportunity to show my dance in a theater setting made me consider the other elements at an earlier stage and forced me to look even deeper at what the raw, basic source of the motivation was in my dance (Ann).

> The fact that we were able to build a final performance in an intimate atmosphere made this class particularly rewarding for me. Not only did this opportunity help me to take myself seriously, but also the response I got from the individuals afterwards made me feel I had truly succeeded in communicating something from inside myself. It affirmed that my experience and view of things was valid (Carol).

Musical Accompaniment

So far nothing has been said about music, and yet we know that music and dance go together. However, if music is introduced too soon, the movement ideas are apt to be influenced by the music rather than emerging from the original intent and intuitive process. As soon as dances begin to hold together as art forms, music should be introduced. This can be done by asking a musician to improvise for the early pieces. The choreographer can perform the work once so the musician gets a feeling for its dynamics and structure. Then repeat the performance with musical accompaniment. The addition of music will usually give a new energy to the performance, heighten the dynamics, and strengthen the continuity and unity inherent in the piece. And, above all, the choreographer gets a feeling of the wholeness of the piece. This early use of improvised musical accompaniment gives the choreographer an opportunity to begin learning about how you collaborate with a composer.

At a later stage of development when students are creating more mature dance forms, there is value in using music more freely. Sometimes this means working with a musician during the process of creating the piece; sometimes it means selecting music that can be used as accompaniment; and other times the dancer might want to work with a specific piece of music from the very beginning.

Summary

When the choreographer is in a state of relaxed concentration and non-ordinary mode of consciousness, an autonomous forming takes over. Scanning the inner scene and searching for order and completion, this autonomous forming process brings sense data and felt thought together in a new synthesis. Emerging from this synthesis is the inner vision that is transformed into the external-ized movement event. The forming process that brings into being the choreography is guided by a concern for simplicity (using only what is needed), unity (interrelated movement), and function (meeting the demands of the situation).

The use of abstract images can be an effective means of stimulat-ing imaginative thought and opening the way for the autonomous forming process to take over. The creative output of each individual will usually pass through several stages of development. The early dance studies tend to be simple in structure and improvisational in nature. With experience, the artistic activity will shift toward more developed forms, moving from the personal to symbolic forms concerned with universal truth.

CHAPTER 7
Self-forming

"You have changed my life. I will never be the same again." I have heard that statement from students so many times. Positive response is always gratifying, but I know that it is not I who changed their life but rather their own experiencing. However, when I hear these comments I always wonder: What is it exactly in the experience that brings about the change in the student?

After observing artistic growth in many students over a long period of time, I have come to believe that when one discovers that inner spirit, and the inner voice is free to make its own unique statement, then something magical happens to the creator. This is especially true when the creative outpourings are respected and valued by others. Suddenly there is a new sense of trust, a confidence in self, and willingness to take greater risks as one reaches toward new artistic goals. As a result, the individual grows creatively and attains a new level of quality and form in choreography.

Art has long been recognized as an important means of expression and communication, but we have not always recognized the significant role that art and the creative process play in self-forming. According to Ernest Schachtel:

> The main motivation at the root of the creative experience is man's need to relate to the world around him. . . . The need is apparent in

the young child's interest in all the objects around him, in his ever renewed exploration and play with them. It is equally apparent in the artist's life long effort to grasp and render something which he has envisioned in his encounter with the world. . . . In such acts of relatedness, man finds both the world and himself (1959: 241).

The choreographer's inner drive to create evolves from the self-world relationship. The act of creating, which involves the total organism, feeds upon the germinal material derived from this intuitive process. The sensing in the body is integrally related to the imaginative thought process and the forming of the aesthetic object. The taking in from the outer world and the giving out, or expressing one's authentic response, is basic to growth as an artist and as a person.

Body Experience: Boundary and Centering

The dance students' feeling of security that frees them to become increasingly self-directed and able to respond with spontaneity is enhanced through sensitive experiencing in the body. It is especially important to have movement experiences that contribute to a strong sense of body boundary and the vertical axis (below/above) and the horizontal axis (in/out). Seymour Fischer has found that "the person with definite boundaries may be assumed to experience what impinges upon him with more perceptual intensity than does the person with indefinite boundaries. . . . With increasing boundary definiteness, a person can more clearly see himself as an individual possessing differentiated identity and can act in a more autonomous and 'self steering' fashion" (1970: 235, 305).

The sense of body boundary is strengthened through stimulation to the outer surface of the body. The dance experience offers opportunity for tactile and kinesthetic sensing that reinforces this sense of boundary. For example, slapping or touching body parts, contact with the environment through pressing against the floor, using your body to push an object, and contracting and releasing tension in the skeletal musculature through progressive relaxation are means of reinforcing a sense of boundary. A strong boundary functions as an interface between the individual and the world. Sensing this demarcation between the inside and outside contributes to the sensing of self: the self that perceives, feels, imagines, and expresses.

Just as a sense of boundary provides a sense of your edge, a sense of center gives a sense of your core. The vertical axis, that line that runs down through the center of the head, through the center of the torso, and down between the legs into the earth, is sensed as the core around which the body parts are integrated. A strong sense of center and its relationship to gravity is a basic factor that affects our ability to balance, to control the body in space, and to interact with our environment. The sense of center frees one to explore out beyond self-space, even take risks, with the assurance that it is possible to return at any time to the security of home base, one's center. This feeling of security makes it possible to interact with more openness and respond with more spontaneity.

The sense of center is discovered first through visualization then is reinforced gradually through movement experiences that involve temporarily shifting and dissolving the center. First there is a sensing of the vertical axis that extends down through the body into the earth. Then the sense of center is strengthened and made functional through developmentally planned movement experiences that range from standing to performing complex movement patterns in space. The following examples illustrate this progression.

Shifting and Dissolving Your Center

- Find your center, then take a step forward shifting center over that foot. Keep the line very straight, then take another step transferring weight but not letting the center break. Repeat.

- Find your center, then shift the weight to one leg so that your center runs down through that leg into the earth. Then shift back with the weight on both feet. Find your center. Now shift to the other leg, being aware of the center. Then back to both feet with the center running down between the legs. Repeat.

- While keeping the center very straight, lean forward as far as possible, then let the body drop but not fall to the floor. Recover balance, returning to a stand. Find your center. Then repeat leaning and losing your balance. Return to upright position with a sense of straight center.

Comment. The reexperiencing of the vertical center following the contrasting sensation of letting go—allowing the center to dissolve temporarily—reinforces the awareness of center. The use of a variety of movement patterns that require shifting balance in different spatial contexts will strengthen the sense of center and make it functional in the larger dance experience.

Body Dimension: The Horizontal and Vertical Axes

Charles Johnston, in his book *The Creative Imperative* (1984), sets forth a model for personal growth that includes two body-oriented dimensions: the vertical axis (below/above) and the horizontal axis (in/out). What he describes as the vertical and horizontal aspects of growth closely parallel what is basic to the creative growth of the choreographer. It would seem that the experiencing of the polarities of the vertical (below/above) and the horizontal (in/out) are not only basic to the process of creating a work of art but also to the organization and growth of the person.

The conflict between the pull of gravity and the desire to ascend to new heights represents the struggle between the safe place and the upward reach of the spirit. This inner drive to ascend is symbolic of growth. A requisite for this kind of upward growth is a sense of being well grounded, having a strong foundation, and being surrounded by an environment that is stimulating and challenging.

Let's look at one example of a movement image that evokes a response symbolic of the inner conflict (below/above) that is present in our personal growth process.

Earth and Heaven

- Mark off your own circle—your own area.

- Walk inside the circle, making smaller and smaller circles until you reach the core of the circle.

- Now feel your feet connected to the earth; feel the pull of gravity into the earth.

- Let the pull take you toward the earth but not so much that you fall. Now recover upward to the standing position.

- Continue exploring the pull of gravity and recovery.

- Now shift the sensations so that you feel the energy coming up from the earth through your body. Feel the energy rising and taking you upward toward the heavens. Explore this upward pull.

- Now explore the pull downward toward the earth and then upward toward the heavens.

- Let this move in any way but keep the concentration on the pull between the downward and the upward; give it freedom to move on its own.

Comment. This exploration of earth and heaven forces the experiencing of the pull between below and above.

The Horizontal Axis

The horizontal axis, with its (in/out) potential for movement, is often taken for granted. However, if these polarities in movement are to become functional, dancers must have an opportunity to explore horizontal movements and progress through a series of developmental stages.

In the early creative exploration in choreography, the tendency is to keep the movement in, or close to the center. This seems to hold true for movement response in various positions: sitting, standing, and moving in space. I have found that images that evoke an outward reach are useful in helping dancers acquire the sensation of moving farther out from the center and becoming comfortable with this outward extending.

Gathering In and Opening Out

- In a sitting or standing position, fold your arms in close to your torso.

- Now let the arms unfold out into space. Repeat, folding in and opening up.

- Have an image of gathering in close to your center. Then releasing and opening out.

- Continue going between gathering in and opening out.

- Explore opening in different directions.

- Be aware of the feeling of bringing in then opening and giving out.

Comment. This in/out way of responding is closely related to the dancer's individual's feeling of closed and open. Being able to respond with receptivity is essential for the taking in from the outer world and giving out in the process of interacting and creating. Another image that is effective in evoking the in/out response is concealing-revealing described in chapter 4.

In the movement experiences, the opening and extending happens first while the dancer is working alone and risking outward explorations evoked by an inner impulse. As the dancer gains confidence, he or she begins to move out from the center and authentic interaction with other dancers gradually develops. These developmental stages of in/out movement seem to parallel the dancers' ability to be receptive and expressive, that is, being open to what they encounter and then making an authentic response.

Summary

These various factors—the vertical axis with the ascending movement, the horizontal axis with the outward reach, and self-directed activity—provide a foundation for the creative act and thus are contributing factors in dancers' creative development and personal growth.

The autonomous act of forming brings about the transformation in the creator's life. Through the creative process, we get in touch with past and present experiences and become deeply involved with feeling, imaging, and forming. While temporarily removed from the everyday world, there is the opportunity to clarify our experiences, to search for truth, and to organize our inner visions. The hidden and unused creative potential comes to life and brings about a personal transformation.

Alwin Nikolais speaks of choreography as a means of self-discovery. Referring to his work, he told me:

> I try to bring out of myself an explanation of who I am and what is my content. By putting that into a shape through motion or a theater piece I explain myself, perhaps with the idea that in explaining myself, I will help others know themselves. In that way we have communication—hopefully a depth of recognition of what life is about.

The very act of creating—giving external form to inner experiencing—seems to have a profound effect upon the discovering and forming of self. This can happen at any stage of development and is not limited to professional artists. It has been said that as one forms in art, one also forms self.

I have listened to students tell me about the way they have changed as a result of the creative experience. I am always moved and a bit in awe of the human potential to change and grow. My goal was to help them release their creative potential and discover a way of working that would result in choreography that was substantive and aesthetically satisfying. And that they did achieve, but, in the process, they also discovered a new sense of self.

These quotes taken from student journals give their own account of personal growth:

> I struggled in the beginning with a general uneasiness. It felt like a weakness—a hole inside of myself. Now that hole has been filled and I am stronger. . . . I feel that just facing myself in class has helped to resolve the stagnation and fear that had hold of me . . . feel more confident, more open, more at ease, and more connected. WOW! That's a lot (Margaret).

> I felt myself as a stranger in the beginning and then my real self

began emerging and did emerge. It is as if a flower had been trying to grow in a mud flat, only to realize upon blossoming, that the flower had been there all along (Audrey).

I feel confident that there is a stronger person emerging as a result of my dancing. Through choreography I have come to realize who I am—a new me has emerged, one that has always been there but just not visible until now (Eunice).

Now there is more strength in my personal character as well as my performance character. This strength builds itself from sensitive findings of that inner self . . . strength that has always been a part of me but not visible to the outside. I started to untap a gold mine in myself that I thought might exist, but wasn't sure.

In class, I was pushed to open up and peer in on what makes me tick. There was another person in me trying to get out and be freed of bondage of the masked persons this world paints on us. Those Fridays of me versus me were most memorable.

Everything culminated for me during a performance . . . suddenly I was moving like being unattached to the mechanics of dance. I was tingling from head to toe with ecstasy. I was truly dancing. I knew then I had moved to a new threshold of feeling. I felt emotions come from the images. What more could you ask in such a short time—only one semester (Samantha).

Creative breakthroughs that result in a new level of artistic achievement are easily recognized, but the subtle inner changes and new perception of self are less apparent to the observer. Revealing statements such as those made by students remind us that the self and the art process are integrally related. As Lewis Mumford has stated:

Art stands as a visible sign of an indwelling in a state of grace and harmony, of exquisite perception and heightened feeling, focused and intensified by the very form into which the artist translates his inner state. This kind of expression is fundamental to man's own sense of himself; it is both self-knowledge and self-realization (1952: 23).

CHAPTER 8

Guiding the
Experiential Process

The focus in the preceding chapters has been on the various aspects of the creative act and ways of facilitating experiences in each. Now we turn our attention to the overall design for the learning experience in choreography.

The structural framework for creative education grows out of your beliefs, the concepts underlying the art experience, and specific goals pertaining to the creative development of individuals. The design for my teaching of choreography is based on two basic beliefs: (1) A learning situation in which the emphasis is on process rather than product would be more effective in fostering students' creative growth; and (2) the presentation and discussion of philosophic and aesthetic concepts relevant to the creative act should be an integral part of the choreographer's experience. I believe that a sound foundation in the process and an understanding of creativity as a mode of human thought and expression will encourage dancers to find their own style, make their unique statements, and ultimately create mature dance forms that are substantive and aesthetically satisfying.

Creative growth takes shape in a spiraling pattern that unfolds through a series of stages or levels. Each new level attained reveals a greater breadth and depth in the understanding of dance as a symbolic form. Each level serves as a foundation and preparation for the next level of growth. Throughout this spiraling growth pattern, the dancer is always involved in the total creative act (feeling, imaging, transforming, and forming). This holds true for the early creative explorations as well as the more advanced work; the process is always the same, but the level of achievement changes. Through the repeated act of creating and making one's statement, the individual grows in choreographic competence. That is why students, from the very beginning, need to have continuing opportunities to create dance studies using their own motivation.

The Spiralling Growth Pattern in Choreography

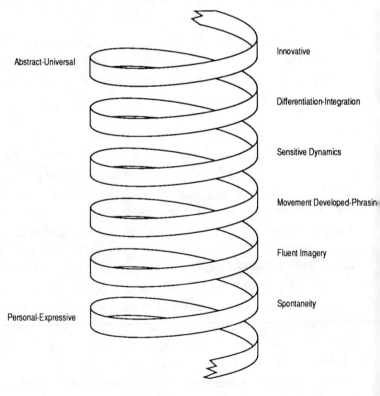

Abstract-Universal

Innovative

Differentiation-Integration

Sensitive Dynamics

Movement Developed-Phrasing

Fluent Imagery

Spontaneity

Personal-Expressive

The Creative Act

An approach to choreography based on holistic layers of learning allows dancers to experience choreographic concepts and elements in the context of the whole. Specifics discovered in this way become more functional. So, instead of presenting principles of composition in a linear fashion through problem-solving tasks, I would wait for new elements of form to occur naturally in the students' work. That is the time to point out the new development and respond with enthusiasm and identify it in relation to a principle of composition. Use the perfect illustration as a means of increasing awareness of a concept so that the new development can be incorporated in the ongoing forming process.

Each individual will progress through the various stages of development at his or her own pace. Sometimes this requires the teacher's understanding and patience. However, the achievement gained through the natural spiraling pattern of growth encourages the beginning dancer and makes possible the progression from beginning to advanced levels: from spontaneous and expressive forms to abstract and sensitively shaped symbolic forms. The challenge for the teacher is to find ways to facilitate experiencing that enriches and enhances the dancers' understanding of each aspect of the process and to do this in the context of the whole.

The overall design assumes that each creative study is a composite of all phases of the process. The levels of achievement will vary, but the process is the same. I see the various aspects of the process (feeling, imaging, transforming, forming) as threads, each of which must be experienced in a developmental fashion but at the same time woven together in such a way that they create a whole: a kind of tapestry that presents the embodiment of the creator's felt experience, imaginative discovery, and inner vision.

The Learning Environment

An environment that supports creative growth is a composite of several factors: the pervading atmosphere, the enrichment that excites and stimulates the learner, and movement experiences that promote creative growth through self-directed activity.

Pervading Atmosphere

The feeling that permeates the learning environment is a critical factor in freeing dancers to explore their imaginative potential. Their first contact with a class not only clarifies the purpose of the course and what is expected of them but also gives a sense of the teacher's commitment and way of working.

During the first meeting, I try to convey my belief that every person has creative potential and that we will be concerned with the discovery and development of this innate ability. I like to engage students in discussion that breaks down the feeling of separation and brings us together as a group. As a means of thinking and sharing of ideas I may ask: Why do you think that people have always danced? Why do you want to make dances? This discussion usually brings forth the idea that people dance to express themselves and to communicate with others. Some say that creating a dance is satisfying. I remember one girl who, after considerable class discussion, said, "I want to create dances in order to better understand myself." As a part of this discussion I usually share one or two statements made by artists about the underlying reason for their creative work.

I make clear that the purpose of the class is to provide them with the opportunity to make their statement through the medium of choreography. I explain that my role is to facilitate and guide the experience. I assure them that I will never do anything that will embarrass them or put them on the spot. We will work in a nonjudgmental environment—never saying that this is right and that is wrong. We will be concerned with sharing, supporting, and learning from each other.

What then *are* my expectations? I say something like this: "I expect you to be committed to your work and to be deeply involved in your own creative process. Learning will evolve from that base. My role will be that of a facilitator and guide. There will be times when things just do not seem to work. This happens to all of

us. No problem. That's part of the process. Don't try to force movement responses, just wait and pick up a little later."

I find that most students have difficulty in believing me when I discuss my approach to the class. They are so accustomed to working in a set structure, where the work is judged as right or wrong, that it is hard to trust this different approach. In order to eliminate their fear and build a trust in our environment, I must truly believe in this nonjudgmental approach with its focus on self-directed activity, and I must be consistent.

It is not only what I say, but also my attitude, body action, and voice that helps to open communication and free students to explore their own feelings and vision. We know that the teacher's voice has great impact on students' responses. When the voice is calm, confident, supportive and flowing with the situation, it helps students let go of fears and tension that block inner-sensing. When the teacher's presence reflects a caring attitude, respect for each individual's effort—never forcing but always helping them discover their potential and find ways to extend themselves—then the students are able to take new risks and set new goals. The nonverbal behavior of the teacher is a powerful force in freeing students and helping them make connections with the inner world of feeling.

Acceptance plays an important role in the learning environment concerned with creative development. Individuals need to feel that their creative work is accepted by peers and teacher. This kind of affirmation assists them in developing a trust in their own ability. This does not mean that praise should be lavished on each piece of creative work. However there is always something good to be found in every creative output, and it can be seen and respected as a step in the direction of growth. This kind of observation helps the teacher and peer group to view each dancer's work in a very personal way: to see new developments, sometimes real breakthroughs. With this focus, the teacher can become sensitive to each student's progress and see what is needed to facilitate the next stage of growth.

Enriched Learning Environment

The ongoing class sessions provide the center for learning. It is here that the students come into contact with ideas, images, and self-directed activity that opens the way for creating their own aesthetic forms.

The choreography class is usually thought of as a place to explore movement, to learn about craft, and to create dances. In other words, the studio is a place to be actively involved in moving and creating while the lecture room is a place to discuss ideas. I believe that in the case of choreography this kind of separation does not make for the best learning situation. Discussion carefully integrated with the ongoing creative work significantly contributes to the understanding of the creative act, deepens the experience, and, in the long run, speeds up students' creative development. Perhaps in our eagerness to be effective we have tended to fragment learning and now need to bring about a better integration of knowledge that supports the creative development of the individual.

A primary goal should be to bring the learner in contact with what is known about creativity as it relates to the human thought process and the symbolization of our experience. This can be achieved in a variety of ways. For example, these topics might be used as a focus for discussion:

1. Arts as a means of expression.

2. Involvement: What does it mean?

3. The role of relaxation in perception and creativity.

4. Feelings—the bodily felt sense.

5. Imaging and imagination.

6. The nature of the creative process.

7. Movement components (space, energy, and rhythm) as aesthetic elements.

8. Two modes of consciousness: logical and intuitive.

9. Form: a human need.

Discussion of these topics can be supported and enriched through the use of:

1. Information from major resources, i.e., Langer, Arnheim, Rugg, Schaeffer-Simmern.

2. Artists' statements about creativity and their process of working.

3. Visual and sound materials that illustrate different aspects of form, i.e., large-size art books, slides of different art forms, recordings of music.

4. Video and film of choreography by professional artists.

Today we have many videos available that show the works of major choreographers of the earlier period, as well as choreographers of the present day. These are important visual resources for choreography students. Video or film can be a valuable means not only of experiencing the style of different artists but also of observing the way they develop the art form. For example, one can observe the opening statement and its development, the use of contrast and dynamics, the energy flow and continuity, the overall unity, and the use of groups. In order for video or film to be most effective, they should be selected in relation to current concerns and used as a way of stimulating the next steps in development. In fact, any presentation and discussion of illustrative material should be carefully related to the students' stage of development. The aim of enrichment is to gain new insight, to open new vistas, and to clarify the needs of the moment.

It is a mistake to think that students are not ready for theoretical and philosophical ideas related to dance until after they have had considerable experience in the studio. On the contrary, students are eager for this kind of information; knowing something about the human experience and artists' creative work makes it easier for them to pursue their own creative work. Here are a few statements made by students about this way of working:

> I like the way we work. It has helped me get into the creative part.
> If we had just done—not talked—I probably would have thought, "What are we doing—I don't understand it."

I like to understand things before I get into them. If it is totally foreign, I feel I can't relate to it.

Since we talk things through ahead of time, it's like "Well that makes sense—I felt free to let go—because there was something connecting" (Michael).

I find the discussions stimulating. I am excited and want to explore what you have just talked about. In previous choreography classes, I was given an assignment, then came in and showed it in class and the work was criticized. I have always wanted to know what was supposed to happen; I wanted to understand the process and learn how to choreograph (Sarah).

Movement Experience

The movement tasks for each class are designed around specific objectives with an eye on immediate concerns as well as long-range development. These experiences should be planned in such a way that the student senses a flow and feeling of development from the opening movement task to the end of the movement session.

In the early work, when the class is more structured and guided, I see the beginning of the class as a time for shifting attention to the present moment of experiencing: attending, inner-sensing, and responding spontaneously. It is a time for opening up and getting in touch with bodily felt sense. Following this initial activity, the focus shifts to movement tasks (always self-directed) that increase awareness of inner-sensing and movement possibilities. For example, the experience might be directed toward becoming aware of feelings or bodily felt sense motivated by word cues such as "heavy," "tightening," "loosening," or the movement task might be concerned with experiencing qualities such as energy, space, and rhythm with their polarities and shadings.

I usually include some kind of interacting with one or more students during the opening section. For example, following an experience based on walking and changing directions—moving fast and slow—I might suggest the following: "When you meet a person, circle around that person so that you are circling around or being encircled. Leave that person, continue moving, meet another person, so that you are always circling or being encircled. Then on to the next person." This is a simple way to introduce relating to another person while still maintaining your sense of involvement.

Another kind of interrelating could follow the exploration of basic movement such as a swing. The following example illustrates the preparation and transition into an improvisation with another person.

- Let the arm swing easily in any direction. Repeat with the other arm easily.

- Now let the arm swing in a curved path; using either arm, feel as though you are carving space.

- Continue letting the curves become larger and larger, moving out into space.

- Now give it freedom to move any way but keep the sensation of curving.

- Let the whole body respond to the curving sensation. Let it develop. Allow time for exploration, then continue.

- At some point, come face-to-face with another person; continue moving in curves keeping the feeling of carving space.

- Let the movement begin to happen in relation to another person; have a sense of interacting.

- Give it freedom to develop on its own.

These interacting experiences with two or more dancers can progress from simple kinesthetic responses to improvisations that evoke a deeper level of feeling and imagination. They will be effective only if students are able to sustain an inner involvement and let movement happen intuitively. Otherwise, they will result in mechanical movement responses that have little value.

Following the opening activity, I like to include a short period of modified progressive relaxation. I have found that carefully guided relaxation helps students gain access to the intuitive mode of consciousness, and to free imagery. I think of the opening portion

of the class, including the relaxation period, as preparation for the more involved creative experience that follows. After relaxation, I begin to build through the use of movement tasks that evoke rich imagery and require a deeper level of involvement. Images are presented in such a way that they lead up to a final movement event. The final image should have potential to draw on previous experience, stimulate images and feelings, and provide the impulse for movement response that unfolds spontaneously and takes its own shape. This is the beginning of the autonomous forming process. As soon as the dancers are ready to pursue their own motivation, I use the last part of the session following relaxation for independent work, but continue to use the first part of class for enrichment and guided explorations of new areas of process.

At the end of the movement session, I like to have the dancers come together, sitting in a circle formation. This is the time to reflect on the day's experience and discuss what happened for them personally. However, there is no pressure to talk; they do this as they are ready. Often the sharing of experience helps the dancers not only to clarify what happened during the movement response but also to see the experience in a larger perspective. Listening to others helps them to see new possibilities and better understand the creative process. My role is primarily one of listening and integrating. I feel that the closing period as well as the discussion at the beginning of class plays a significant role in establishing a feeling of trust and sense of community.

The structure of the choreography class provides for an integration of philosophic and aesthetic ideas, creative movement experience, and a time for reflection at the close of the session. In order for the learning to be structured in this way, an adequate block of time must be provided. I find that two and one-half to three hours is needed for this kind of in-depth experience.

Advanced Study

The primary emphasis throughout this book has been on the creative process and its relationship to the creating of dance forms.

The movement tasks used to illustrate this way of working are discussed in relation to the early experiences. Little has been said about advanced work in choreography. So one might ask: What is the relationship of the fundamental approach as described to the ongoing work of the artist-choreographer?

Obviously the images and movement experiences must be adapted as the student progresses so that they are appropriate for the current level of work. However, I have found that many of the images that have been suggested can be effective at different levels of experience. Advanced students will use the image as a starting point and then go on to respond intuitively at a deeper level.

A major difference between beginning and advanced experience is the proportion of time spent on independent work. Much of the early experience is facilitated by the teacher. Experiences are designed to stimulate self-directed response and enhance under-standing of the creative process and the nature of movement as an expressive medium. Gradually, the emphasis shifts so that the dancers' creative work, stimulated by their own motivation, be-comes the primary activity. The emphasis is on making their state-ment. Even at this level, some use of images—such as those described in the section on improvisation—is valuable, just to keep them in touch with the intuitive process.

As a choreographer gains experience and increased competence, there is always a danger of being tempted to turn out dances quickly. This usually means resorting to an intellectual approach as a means of organizing movement. When this happens, the em-phasis shifts to product and the fundamental creative process ceases to function. Regardless of the level of work, the true creative process depends on getting in touch with an inner source—inner listening—and allowing movement to flow from that inner source. This way of working takes time but is essential if the choreography is to have a sense of authenticity and present the truth as the artist sees it. As Sybil Shearer has said: "The seed has to be real in order for the plant to grow" (1988: 35).

Advanced students in a class situation need to be able to work in a flexible time schedule that allows the choreography to develop organically. Unrealistic deadlines for final showing can be disastrous to the basic process. In an attempt to meet external expectations, students often shift to intellectual planning. Of course this usually results in choreography that may be technically good but lacking in substance and authenticity. The choreographer must have time for the idea to germinate and the external form to emerge as the autonomous forming process takes shape. Sometimes this happens rather quickly, but other times the final form emerges slowly.

Teachers can contribute to the expanding and deepening of advanced students' understanding of the choreographic process in several ways. Short-term projects can be designed so that they stimulate the dancer to explore new approaches to choreographic ideas and forms. These might be directed toward a new exploration of movement ideas, experiencing more in depth, becoming aware of different approaches to form, or increasing competence in certain aspects of craft as they relate to the choreographic process. Carefully structured projects will stimulate the dancers to extend themselves in new directions and also provide an excellent framework for discussion. The follow-up discussion brings the inherent concepts, principles, and approaches to a conscious level. These guided experiences should parallel and supplement the dancers' ongoing creative work based on their own motivation.

These exercises illustrate the use of guided experiences to help dancers deepen their understanding of movement potential and the forming process in dance making.

Soaring, Turning, Descending (group of five or more)

- While standing, let the body and arms move in curving patterns.
- Keep the feeling of curves and begin walking in circular paths.
- Let the curves carry you into circles: small circles, large circles.
- Let the curved sensation take you into turning: slow, fast, large, small.

- Let the movement stop gradually.
- Feel your feet connected to the floor.
- Sense the energy coming up from the earth, through the legs, torso, and arms.
- Repeat the upward flow of energy. Have the feeling of being lifted.
- Begin to move in space. Feel the energy rising up through the torso and out through the arms.
- Now have the feeling of soaring—rising up higher and higher.
- Now let it descend.
- Continue exploring the feeling of soaring and descending.
- Stop for a moment but keep your concentration.
- Now combine the three feelings: soaring, turning, descending.
- Let it move spatially and develop on its own: sometimes soaring, sometimes turning, sometimes descending.
- Try to keep a sense of flow and continuity.
- Let it find its own ending.

Comment. The focus of this improvisation is on spatial exploration, transitions, and continuity.

Two as One *(group of two)*

- Stand facing another person.
- Let the torso sway gently while mirroring each other as in a mirror image.
- Let the torso begin to rotate and the arms swing easily.
- One person may initiate new movement. The other person responds as in a mirror image.
- Let the movement and interaction develop.
- At some point, one person moves away to explore movement independently.
- The other person explores his or her own identity.
- Sometimes you are drawn back together and move in unison.

- Continue exploring the desire for separate identity and the pull toward moving in unison.
- Let it find its own ending.

Comment. This improvisation could provide the foundation for the study of the duet as a dance form.

Facade (group of five or more)

Preparation. Have students observe people in different situations: on the street, in the shops, at work. Observe their facial expressions and body attitudes. Do individuals appear involved with the environment or do they seem removed from it? Do they appear to be wearing a mask that separates the *me* from *out there?* Study their body attitudes, interactions with others, and movement expressions.

In the following class, have students discuss what they saw and sensed about people: their attitudes and their responses to other people. Follow up the discussion with an improvisation.

- Take a position somewhere in the room: kneeling, standing, or sitting.
- Have the image of the studio as a large stage filled with people who are going about their daily activities.
- When you are ready, start moving to other areas of the stage. As you pass people, show little awareness of them.
- Continue moving in different directions, meeting and passing as in everyday life.
- Move with a feeling of being self-contained. Keep your facade.
- Let the movement develop on its own.
- Feel the intensity of the situation increasing.
- Perhaps someone breaks out of this pattern. Is there a desire for interaction? Do others respond or keep their facade?
- Take your time. Let the movement happen on its own.
- Let it go until it finds its own resolution.

Comment. This improvisation could provide material for a group dance, *Facade*, based on the human experience of isolation and aloneness.

Inner Conflict (solo)

Preparation. Provide students with large sheets of paper and chalk of different colors.

• Sit in a comfortable position. Select a piece of chalk.

• Let the chalk move rapidly over the paper, filling it with color.

• Take a clean sheet of paper. This time have the feeling of being unsure: tentative, fumbling, floundering. Select a color. Let the feeling guide the movement of the chalk.

• Take a clean sheet. This time have the feeling of inner strength: strong and in control. Select a color. Let the drawing just happen.

• Look at the two sheets. Notice the difference in energy and spatial patterns.

• Take a standing position somewhere in the room.

• Walk off two fairly large circles, side by side, with space in between.

• Step inside of one circle.

• Have the image that each circle has a different feeling. In one there is the feeling of being unsure, fumbling, and floundering. In the other circle, there is the feeling of inner strength, power, and being in control.

• When you are ready, let the movement begin to happen in response to the feeling in your circle.

• Gradually you are pulled into the other circle. Let the movement happen in response to the different feeling.

• Have the image of a person struggling between the pull of two different feelings.

• Let the movement develop in each circle but always being aware of the pull between them.

• Let it develop and then come to an ending.

Comment. This improvisation draws on the movement response to contrasting feeling states. The movement ideas could be developed as a solo dance, *Unresolved Conflict.*

Another way of enriching the learning environment for advanced students is through the use of visual materials: dance films, videos, and other art forms such as paintings, sculpture, and photography. The way that these materials may be related to the ongoing work was discussed in chapter 7. The viewing of live concerts by professional artists should be an integral part of the student's experience. Through these encounters, they experience the metaphoric use of movement to create illusion and discover dance as a profound means of communication.

Perhaps some of the most significant learning experiences for the more advanced choreographers takes place through their own creative work. First there is the inner or intuitive process and sometimes struggle to bring the work to fruition. Then there is the sharing of the work in progress and the follow-up discussion. At this point the choreographer wants to have the reactions and suggestions from observers: Was the intent clear? Did the work hold together? Were there sections that were weak or unrelated?

As in the evaluative process, it is important that the response and discussion be handled in a positive and supportive manner. If this kind of relationship has existed throughout, the teacher and student will have established a mutual trust that makes it possible for the teacher to be more direct and specific with suggestions. This is the time when the teacher's knowledge and experience can be shared more freely. However, the teacher's first obligation is to sense what the choreographer is trying to achieve. Then, questions are asked and suggestions are made, but never in a way that takes the control away from the choreographer. This is why the attitude of sharing is so important. Ideally one tries to give honest reactions and open up new ideas for the choreographer to explore. But this should never be done in a way that makes the choreographer feel that the teacher is remaking the dance in relation to his or her perception and imagination.

The advanced choreographer will find that frequent videotaping is an excellent means of assessing the ongoing work. This makes it possible to observe the movement material and its development with a critical eye. Also, it affords the opportunity to respond to the work at the feeling level and assess its aesthetic impact. The teacher's suggestion for observation will help sharpen the choreographer's awareness of sections that need additional work.

The goal is to enrich the environment in ways that assist dancers in the development of their creative potential through the medium of choreography, through guided improvisation, discussions, visual materials, and observations. But throughout the experience, from beginning through advanced work, there must be a continuous thread of self-directed creative work flowing from the dancers' own motivation. This is the primary means of enhancing their understanding of the art process; it enables them to create with increased sensitivity and sophistication. The challenge is to keep alive the basic intuitive process so fundamental in the creative act, while continuing to broaden and deepen understanding of form and the use of movement as universal means of symbol making and communication. As one teacher aptly put it:

> I wanted to be in this class because there was something wrong with the way that I was teaching choreography, and I was not seeing the reasons. I felt that watching a master teacher at work with basically the same level of students that I have would give me insight into another approach to teaching and guiding beginning students through the creative process. I viewed several videotapes of Dr. Hawkins' choreography students at a conference sometime ago, and was deeply impressed with the quality of the movement and genuineness of expression in those first dance studies. Hopefully I would learn the approach she uses and be able to understand my students better.
>
> Choreography has always been easy for me. I think that is why it has been difficult to teach. I do not know what it is that blocks and embarrasses and eventually short-circuits the creative process, especially in beginning students. It is through the basic understanding of the whole process as it works in all people that I came to know the stages one must pass through in order to bring it to a perfor-

mance level. Gently guiding with no judgmental remarks along the way to force understanding, but accepting small insights from each individual at whatever level they come from and introducing bit by bit another level of perception is the way to teach choreography. I have learned to listen and look more to the things that my students are saying and doing so that I can guide them from where they are to the next level. I have learned to wait for them to process other kinds of experiences with what I present as possibilities and to integrate all of those into their own movement expression.

Because of this class and my experience in it, I have improved my teaching of choreography. Evidence of this fact is the group of final dances that I viewed last month. They were by far the best finals I have seen in any of my years of teaching (Janet).

CHAPTER 9

Evaluating

Stepping back to take a look at what we have created is as natural a part of the creative act as the original impulse to give outer shape to the inner vision. Just as the artist, during the creative process, goes back and forth between the outer objectification and inner vision, there is a similar impulse to assess our creative output after the completion of a piece or even segments of a larger work. The creator has a need to see if the objectified form is true to the inner vision. Does the art work make apparent the real intent? Does the unfolding movement create a dynamic play of interacting forces that result in the desired illusion—an underlying metaphoric statement?

Because self-assessment is a basic tendency of the creative person, the teacher must consider the students' innate potential for self-evaluation as well as the teacher's role as facilitator in the evaluative process. Certainly evaluation is an integral part of the learning process. The question is: how to use it most effectively?

If the goal for young choreographers, especially during their early experiences, is to free the imagination, build self-confidence, and encourage risk taking, then the locus of evaluation should be internal, not external. In other words, the creator should play a primary role in assessing the newly created forms. If we accept that concept, then what is the role of the teacher?

The teacher, without violating the belief that the focus of evaluation should be internal, can use the observation period as an opportunity to assist dancers in seeing their work more clearly and increasing their awareness of various elements of form. This is a time for indirect teaching. Through the use of guidelines for observation and carefully framed questions and comments about new developments—real breakthroughs—the teacher assists the choreographer in discovering what is happening in the movement event, clarifying what is desired, and gaining insight about how to achieve that goal. Through this indirect approach, which does not take control away from the creator, the teacher contributes enormously to the dancers' creative growth and the development of their innate potential for self-evaluation.

Using Videotape as a Tool for Evaluation

Videotaping of the individual's creative work (fragments, studies, and completed dances) provides the choreographer with an extremely valuable means of observing work in process and making self-assessment. During this time of viewing and assessing, the teacher acts as facilitator in the process of seeing, sensing, and gaining new insight about the forming process.

Students who have not worked with video may feel self-conscious and hesitant about having their performance recorded. In fact, students will have some feeling of fear the first time they are asked to show their work in class. So the teacher, being aware of these personal concerns, can prepare students so that the first experiences are less disturbing and are seen as a time for them to try out their material.

As soon as students are creating short studies that may be based on suggested images or on their own motivation, I find it helpful to have them share their work with the class. This showing can be introduced by having half of the class perform at the same time while the other half observes. The purpose is to give dancers a chance to perform their own work and to see what others are doing. This approach makes a safe environment for the first showings. Next, I would have smaller groups performing, and finally individuals would take turns showing their work. When individuals perform one at a time, they have a chance to explore the spatial context of their dance. The audience can see detail more clearly and follow the continuity of the unfolding event.

In these early showings, it is important that the response to each dancer's work be positive and supportive. It is a time to point out interesting moments in the movement and new developments. Above all, the creator needs to feel that his or her work is accepted and respected. During these showings, it is important to establish an environment that helps dancers develop a feeling of trust.

The first time the video camera is used, it is important to discuss the plan for the day. I would explain that the purpose of recording is to give them an opportunity to see their work-in-progress: "When you are moving you know how it feels but you can't see it from the outside. The videotape makes it possible to see what you have created, to experience the movement event as it unfolds, and to assess the externalized form in relation to your image, inner-sensing, and intent." In order to keep an informal atmosphere while we are recording, I suggest that they take turns, one after the other, but let each person decide when to perform. In other words, I would not call on people or present an order, but instead let them assume that responsibility.

When recording is completed, there should be an immediate playback. Ideally the tape should be stopped after each study so that the creator has a chance to react immediately and others have an opportunity to share in the discussion. If time does not permit stopping after each piece, then wait and view the entire tape. The follow-up discussion is valuable, but it is difficult to respond to each piece as specifically as in the other approach.

Class Discussion

The effectiveness of observation and follow-up discussion is affected significantly by the way the teacher enters into the process. Obviously the dancers will be interested in seeing the results of their work and will make their own assessment. But the teacher can add another dimension to the experience by providing one or two simple guidelines that will help the choreographer focus and see the work more clearly. Of course, these suggestions should be made in relation to the dancers' level of development.

For example, at the time of the first showing, I would be especially interested in the dancers' ability to stay involved so that the externalized movement reflects an inner-sensing. In other words, the movement event, no matter how simple or short, conveys a sense of authenticity. Before the viewing, I might say something like this: "Let's get a feel of the whole study but pay special attention to the level of involvement. Is the movement involved? Are there times when it is not involved?" This kind of guideline helps them discover the difference between movement that is truly involved, integrally connected with inner-sensing, and movement that is intellectually planned or manipulated without any sense of inner vitality.

Suggestions for focusing the attention at follow-up showings might include:

Does it have a feeling of continuity?

Does it have a beginning, develop, go somewhere, and end?

What about the dynamics? Is there a change in the quality?

Is the whole body involved?

Do you sense an underlying rhythm?

How is the space used?

As the work progresses, the guidelines would reflect different aspects of the form:

Is there more than one section? If so, is there a flow from one section to the other?

Are the movement ideas developed?

Does the movement build in intensity then resolve? Is there an overall sense of unity?

These questions illustrate how you could make suggestions that relate to the current level of work. Through this kind of focused observation, the choreographer gains an understanding of form concepts: simplicity, continuity, dynamics, and unity. By using one or two guidelines for each viewing, the choreographer has a chance to become aware of the progress that has been made and also the need for development in certain areas.

The Teacher's Role

How the teacher enters into the follow-up discussion depends to some extent on his or her personality and background. Let me give a brief description of the approach that I have found to be effective in guiding the evaluative process. Following the viewing of an individual study, I would ask the creator to respond to the work. I might start discussion by asking: "How did you feel about it? Did it look the way you thought it would?" After the individual has had a chance to think about the work and respond, I might ask a question or make a comment in relation to the particular guideline that I had given earlier. For example, if a comment had been made that the movement did not stay involved throughout I might ask: "Where did you feel that the movement lost involvement? When did it become involved again?"

In later showings, when dancers are exploring new movement ideas, I try to stay alert to their development and point them out. This gives the creator encouragement and contributes to everyone's increased understanding of the choreographic process. For example, the following kind of comments might grow out of what I see:

- I notice that you use your body more fully than any time before— the arms, legs, and torso were all involved. That was exciting!
- Were you aware that you moved out into space in new ways? Your

movement gave a spatial context that added an important dimension to the work.

- Did you notice how the opening movement caught your attention and immediately pulled you into the work? Then the following movement unfolded and grew out of that opening statement. That was an important new development for you!

Comments such as these help to focus the attention and open the way for discussion of a new use of movement or specific element of form, and indirectly contribute to new awareness and insight.

As the dancer progresses to more advanced work and a mutual trust has been established, the questions and comments can relate more specifically to weak spots in the choreography. For example, I might say:

- I wonder about the next to last section of the movement? Does it break the continuity that you are trying to create?

- Does the resolution feel right to you?

- You might want to explore the section that moves in a circular path. What would happen if you kept the same movement idea but varied the dynamics?

The idea is to help dancers identify problem areas and find solutions. In an unobtrusive way, you try to focus attention on specific aspects of the work and encourage the dancers to draw from greater depths of experience.

I see the video observations as a time for dancers to assess the work-in-progress and see how the performance relates to the intent behind the movement. As one student stated:

Working with the video made it easier for me to see what worked and what didn't work. All your helpful questions and hints about rhythm, space, flow, and contrast were leading me to a better understanding of how to look at the raw material, how to form it into a finished dance—or better towards the form that I am pleased with.

I feel that I am on the right track, still in the beginning indeed, but I have received answers to some of my questions. Gradually I got a deeper insight into the whole process. And I have learned what I simply have to do, with all the beginner's difficulties. I have to go step-by-step. The safe environment encouraged me to trust myself and to work at my own pace (Judy).

This discussion of evaluation was centered around the use of video. I believe that the opportunity to view the recording of student work is an important phase in the learning process. However, if video equipment is not available or if it is not used for every showing, the basic process would be the same. I would still use the same kind of viewing guidelines and respond to the showing with similar questions.

Summary

Having an opportunity to perform and then view what has been created is an integral aspect of artistic activity. The creator is interested in assessing the short study or complete dance in terms of the original intent and inner vision. This is a time for assessment and for gaining insight about the forming process. Also, it is a time for sharing the work with others. In order for this experience to be an effective part of the learning process, it must happen in an atmosphere that conveys a feeling of acceptance and respect for each dancers' work.

The creator should play a primary role in the assessment process. The locus of evaluation should be internal not external. The teacher's role is one of providing a focus for the observation, recognizing significant developments, and then using these breakthroughs as a basis for indirect teaching about some aspect of form.

The effectiveness of an indirect approach to learning depends on the teacher's ability to see clearly and respond creatively. The intent, underlying the suggested questions and comments related to the student's creative work, is a concern for teaching in a way that facilitates experiencing, discovering, and creative growth. Through the indirect approach, the dancers are encouraged to develop their innate sense of form and create dances that are organic and aesthetically satisfying.

For example, instead of teaching specific principles of composition and design and then assigning studies that make use of specific principles, I would wait until the perfect illustration appears in the creative outpouring of some student. Then I would seize that moment to point it out and discuss it in relation to craftsmanship, suggesting that it is something that is useful to know. In this way, the creator and the class become aware of what the experienced artist knows as the principles of composition. Of course this assumes that one believes that all people have an innate sense of form, and with the appropriate experiences that enrich the learning environment, the externalized form will gradually evolve and mature.

In order to be successful with an indirect approach to learning, the teacher must stay deeply involved in the process and be able to respond spontaneously to the significant moments in the dancer's creative output. When a specific aspect of the work is praised and discussed, the learner gains new awareness of his or her creative potential as well as the nature of the forming process. Hugh Mearns, the distinguished teacher of creative writing, describes good teaching in this way: "Primarily, it is the job of uncovering native gifts of insight, feeling, and thinking" (1958: 267).

CHAPTER 10

Epilogue

At a time when dance is in transition, which it clearly is today, we need to turn our attention to its basic source of vitality. We need to rediscover the roots of this body-oriented means of expression and its relation to the creative thought process.

The arts always reflect the life of a society and the special happenings of any particular period. Certainly this is true of dance. For example, the unprecedented level of technical virtuosity displayed by contemporary artists surely reflects the technological developments in today's world. There are times when it seems that the main function of a piece of choreography is to display the technical ability of the performer. Also, there can be little doubt that the materialistic values and feelings of disconnectedness that we experience every day are powerful forces that influence our expression. Sometimes the choreographic response to these forces seems to aim at the level of entertainment or innovations that present novelty for its own sake.

In our effort to find new outlets for our expression, there is always the danger of losing contact with the formative process that transforms the personal experience and imbues it with a life of its own. When this happens, the thought process shifts from process to product. We lose contact with the inner experiencing and creative thought process that taps into the imaginative, intuitive, and symbolic levels of knowing.

So, from time to time, we are challenged to get back in touch with our roots, to reexperience what has been called *basic dance*, and to recognize the body as a vehicle for feeling, a fundamental way of knowing. When we are in tune with this level of understanding of human potential, the art form emanates from our inner experiencing and radiates its own vitality. The choreography, when performed, transcends the movement event and presents a metaphoric image of human experience.

My approach to dance making attempts to reawaken the inner resources available to every person. Through self-directed experiences, dancers are encouraged to discover their potential for creativity and to engage in the formative process that makes possible the coming into being of new entities or dances that have a sense of vitality and authenticity.

In this time of transition, our society should value and nurture this kind of artistic activity for all persons, not only the emerging artists. Through the creative experience, the individual gains self-knowledge and a way of thinking that enriches his or her life and the culture as a whole.

Appendix

Progressive Relaxation

(This is a modified version. For a full description of progressive relaxation, see McGuigan [1981] and Jacobson [1976].)

Position: Lying on the floor, legs straight, arms resting by the sides.

Arm

- Bend the hand of one arm back at the wrist, fingers pointing upward. Hold briefly. Locate the tension signal (upper front of the arm).
- Relax the tension signal; power off. Let the hand and arm go limp.
- Repeat two times.
- Turn hand forward toward body. Locate the tension signal (bottom forearm).
- Relax the tension signal.
- Repeat two times.
- Repeat the up and in movement with the other arm.

Leg

- Bend the foot of one leg upward, toes toward ceiling. Hold briefly. Locate the tension signal (front of lower leg).

- Relax the tension signal; foot falls and leg goes limp.

- Repeat two times.

- Extend the foot forward. Hold briefly. Locate tension signal (in calf).

- Repeat two times.

- Repeat the upward bend and extension with the other leg.

Abdominal Area

- Tighten the abdominal area. Locate the tension signal (upper abdominal area).

- Relax the tension signal.

- Repeat two times.

Shoulder Area

- Bend shoulders back, toward the spine. Locate the tension signal (between shoulders).

- Relax the tension signal.

- Repeat two times.

Face

- Wrinkle forehead upward. Locate the tension signal (upper forehead).

- Relax tension signal.

- Repeat two times.

- Frown pulling forehead muscles down. Locate tension signal (between eyes).

- Relax tension signal.

- Repeat two times.

- Close jaws tightly. Locate tension signal (back of lower jaw).
- Relax tension signal.
- Repeat two times.

Each phase should be performed slowly. Concentrate on becoming aware of the delicate tension signal. Wait briefly before repeating the action. These movements should not be performed as exercises. The focus is on feeling the tension signal, then releasing at that spot.

Transition to Follow-up Movement

Use some image or movement that assists in making the transition from the relaxed state to readiness for the next movement experience. For example:

Image

- Have the image of a string attached to your wrist. It is being pulled upward, lifting your arm without any effort on your part. Feel it being lifted in any direction.
- Then the arm descends.
- Repeat several times.
- Shift to the other arm; feel it being lifted, then descending.
- Repeat several times.
- This time let the lifting of your arm take you into a sitting position. (Then proceed with the next activity.)

Bibliography

Adams, Ansel, with Mary Street Alinder. *Ansel Adams: An Autobiography.* Boston: Little, Brown, 1985.

Anderson, Harold H., ed. *Creativity and Its Cultivation.* New York: Harper and Brothers, 1959.

Bogen, Joseph E. "The Other Side of the Brain: An Appositional Mind." In *The Nature of Human Consciousness,* edited by Robert E. Ornstein. New York: Viking, 1974.

————. "Some Educational Aspects of Hemispheric Specialization." In *UCLA Educator,* edited by M. C. Wittrock. Los Angeles: Overland, 1975.

Bruner, Jerome. *On Knowing: Essays for the Left Hand.* New York: Atheneum, 1965.

Campbell, Joseph, with Bill Moyers. *The Power of Myth.* New York: Doubleday, 1988.

Cohen, Selma Jeanne, ed. *The Modern Dance: Seven Statements of Belief.* Middletown, CT: Wesleyan University Press, 1965.

Copland, Aaron. *Music and Imagination.* New York: Mentor, 1959.

Deikman, Arthur J. "Bi-Modal Consciousness." In *The Nature of Human Consciousness,* edited by Robert E. Ornstein. New York: Viking, 1974.

Dow, Alden B. "An Architect's Views on Creativity." In *Creativity and Its Cultivation*, edited by Harold H. Anderson. New York: Harper and Brothers, 1959.

Fein, Sylvia. *Heidi's Horse*. Pleasant Hill, CA: Exelrod Press, 1976.

Fischer, Seymour. *Body Experience in Fantasy and Behavior*. New York: Appleton, Century, Crofts, 1970.

Gardner, Howard. *Art, Mind, and Brain*. New York: Basic Books, 1982.

———. *Frames of Mind: The Theory of Multiple Intelligences*. New York: Basic Books, 1983.

Ghiselin, Brewster, ed. *The Creative Process*. Berkeley: University of California Press, 1952.

Hawkins, Alma M. *Creating Through Dance*. 2nd ed. Princeton: Dance Horizons/Princeton Book Co., 1988.

H'Doubler, Margaret N. *Dance: A Creative Art Experience*. Madison: University of Wisconsin Press, 1957.

Henri, Robert. *The Art Spirit*. New York: McGraw-Hill, 1960.

Jacobson, Edmund. *You Must Relax*. New York: McGraw-Hill, 1976.

Jenkins, Iredell. *Art and the Human Enterprise*. Cambridge: Harvard University Press, 1958.

Johnson, Charles. *The Creative Imperative*. Berkeley: Celestial Arts, 1984.

Kubie, L. S. *Neurotic Distortion of the Creative Process*. New York: Farrar, Strauss & Giroux, 1942.

Langer, Susanne K. *Philosophy in a New Key*. Cambridge: Harvard University Press, 1942.

———. *Feeling and Form*. New York: Charles Scribner's Sons, 1953.

———. *Problems of Art*. New York: Charles Scribner's Sons, 1957.

Louis, Murray. *Inside Dance*. New York: St. Martins Press, 1980.

McGuigan, F. J. *Calm Down: A Guide for Stress and Tension Control*. Englewood Cliffs, NJ: Prentice-Hall, 1981.

Malraux, André. *Voices of Silence*. Garden City, NY: Doubleday, 1953.

Martin, John. *Introduction to the Dance.* New York: W. W. Norton, 1939.

May, Rollo. *The Courage to Create.* New York: W. W. Norton, 1975.

Mearns, Hugh. *Creative Power.* New York: Dover Publications, 1958.

Moore, Henry. "Notes on Sculpture." In *The Creative Process,* edited by Brewster Ghiselin. Berkeley: University of California Press, 1952.

Morgan, Barbara, ed. *Barbara Morgan.* Hastings on Hudson, NY: Morgan and Morgan, 1972.

Mumford, Lewis. *Art as Technic.* New York: Columbia University Press, 1952.

O'Keeffe, Georgia. *Georgia O'Keeffe: A Studio Book.* New York: Viking, 1976.

Ornstein, Robert E., ed. *The Psychology of Consciousness.* New York: Viking, 1972.

———. *The Nature of Human Consciousness.* New York: Viking, 1974.

Richards, M. C. *Centering: Poetry, Pottery and the Person.* New York: Columbia University Press, 1962.

———. *The Crossing Point.* Middletown, CT: Wesleyan University Press, 1973.

Rogers, Carl. "Towards a Theory of Creativity." In *Creativity and Its Cultivation,* edited by Harold H. Anderson. New York: Harper and Brothers, 1959.

Rugg, Harold. *Imagination.* New York: Harper & Row, 1963.

Samuels, Mike, and Mary Samuels. *Seeing with the Mind's Eye.* New York: Random House, 1975.

Schachtel, Ernest G. *Metamorphosis.* New York: Basic Books, 1959.

Schaeffer-Simmern, Henry. *The Unfolding of Artistic Activity.* Berkeley: University of California Press, 1961.

Shahn, Ben. *The Shape of Content.* New York: Random House, 1957.

Shearer, Sybil. "John Martin, A Tribute." *Ballet Review* 16:1.

Sinnott, Edmund. "The Creativeness of Life." In *Creativity and Its Cultivation*, edited by Harold H. Anderson. New York: Harper and Brothers, 1959.

Smith, Paul, ed. *Creativity*. New York: Hastings House, 1959.

Sokolow, Anna. "The Rebel and the Bourgeois." In *The Modern Dance: Seven Statements of Belief*, edited by Selma Jeanne Cohen. Middletown, CT: Wesleyan University Press, 1965.

Sperry, R. W., M. S. Gazzaniga, and J. E. Bogan. "Interhemispheric Relationships: The Neocortical Commissures; Syndromes of Hemispheric Disconnection." In *Handbook of Clinical Neurology*, edited by P. J. Vinken and G. W. Bruyn. Amsterdam: North Holland Publishing Co., 1969.

Wigman, Mary. *The Language of Dance*. Middletown, CT: Wesleyan University Press, 1966.